Elvis

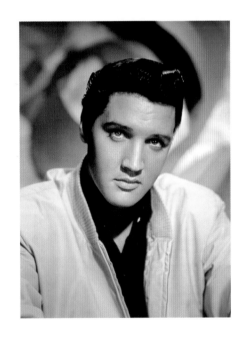

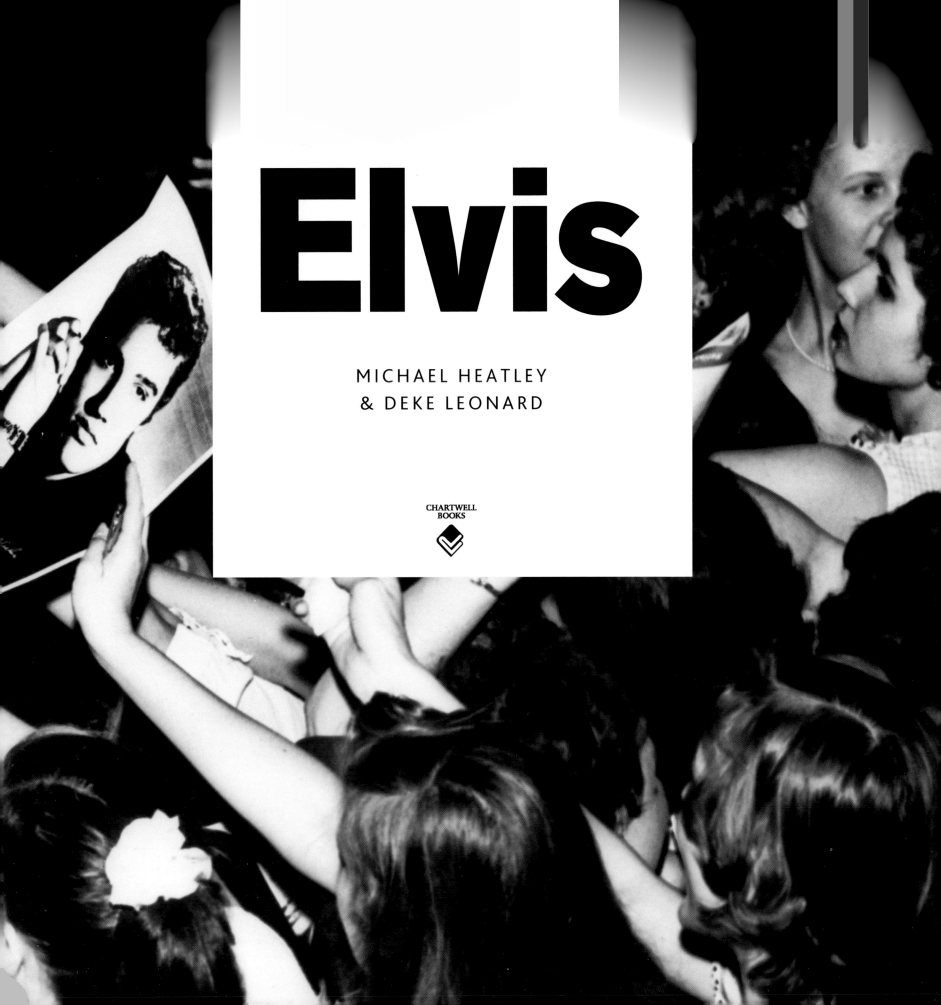

Elvis

MICHAEL HEATLEY
& DEKE LEONARD

CHARTWELL
BOOKS

This edition published in 2014 by

CHARTWELL BOOKS
an imprint of Book Sales
a division of Quarto Publishing Group USA Inc.
276 Fifth Avenue Suite 206
New York, New York 10001
USA

ISBN-13: 978-0-7858-3172-3

Printed and bound in China

PHOTOGRAPHY

Every effort has been made to trace the copyright holders. Greene Media Ltd. apologizes for any unintentional omissions, and would be pleased, if any such case should arise, to add an appropriate acknowledgement in future editions. The Publisher would like to thank all those at Corbis, Getty Images and Topfoto who helped with the photo research.

ANSWERS TO QUIZ
QUESTIONS ON PAGE 190

1. Jesse Garon Presley
2. 1958
3. $100,000
4. 1954
5. Jerry Lee Lewis, Carl Perkins, Johnny Cash
6. Arthur Crudup's "That's Alright (Mama)"
7. Eleven
8. 1968
9. Six
10. Holland
11. 1971
12. Friedberg, Germany
13. 1995
14. "Blue Suede Shoes"
15. Sergeant
16. Elvis Sings The Wonderful World of Christmas
17. NBC
18. His Hand in Mine
19. Elvis' Christmas Album
20. Clint Reno
21. Change Of Habit
22. Twenty
23. 2007
24. Moody Blue
25. 1968
26. Best Sacred Performance for "How Great Thou Art"
27. 1967
28. Beaulieu
29. The International Convention Center Arena in Honolulu
30. Indianapolis, Indiana
31. A Bueau of Narcotics and Dangerous Drugs badge
32. 1999
33. 1955
34. $40,000
35. Today
36. 1975
37. Fourteen
38. Bill Black, DJ Fontana, and Scotty Moore
39. 149
40. Eighteen
41. Best Inspirational Performance' for "He Touched Me"
42. 1998
43. 1991
44. Forty-seven
45. Viva Las Vegas
46. August 18, 1977
47. 1973
48. The Golden Globe Award for Best Documentary Film
49. "If I Can Dream'
50. Audubon Drive

COVER PHOTOGRAPHS:
FRONT COVER: Paramount Pictures/Collection Sunset Boulevard/Corbis 42-23493104

CD: Metro-Goldwyn-Mayer/Sunset Boulevard/Corbis 42-25492865

BACK COVER: Michael Ochs Archives/Corbis 42-17853565

PAGE 1: Elvis Presley, 1965. *Bettmann/Corbis U1464166*

PAGE 2–3: Elvis Presley surrounded by his enthusiastic teenage fans, 1956. *Bettmann/Corbis BE047916*

RIGHT AND ON CHAPTER OPENERS: *Topfoto ulls046675*

Contents

Chapter 1

Elvis's Early Life

"I was training to be an electrician. I suppose I got wired the wrong way round somewhere along the line." ~ Elvis Presley

BIRTHPLACE OF
ELVIS PRESLEY

Elvis Aaron Presley was born Jan. 8, 1935, in this house, built by his father. Presley's career as a singer and entertainer redefined American popular music. He died Aug. 16, 1977, at Memphis, Tennessee.

LEFT: The Tupelo, Mississippi house where Elvis was born on January 8, 1935.
Philip Gould/Corbis PG004534

ELVIS'S EARLY LIFE

"I didn't know what I wanted to do as a kid. But I used to pray to God that I'd amount to something some day. I never dreamed that something like this would happen." ~ **Elvis Presley**

The birth of Elvis Aaron Presley in his family's shotgun shack in Tupelo, Mississippi, soon after midday on January 8, 1935, lit the touch paper on a musical and cultural revolution. That revolution continues to this day, three and a half decades after his death and over half a century since he first hit the charts.

Gladys Presley had been expecting twins and, after Elvis was safely born, a twin brother emerged—sadly, he was never to breathe. Formally named Jesse Garon, he would be buried the following day in an unmarked grave on a nearby hillside cemetery. Elvis was later to say of his stillborn sibling: "Many folk believe that when one twin dies the other grows up with all the qualities of the other. If that did happen to me, then I'm lucky."

Father Vernon had constructed the family home after learning Gladys was pregnant, borrowing $180 from his then employer, a farmer, for materials and building it with assistance from his brother and father. Gladys had been earning $2 an hour at a local garment-producing company when she was working, so these were humble beginnings for the youngster by any yardstick. Yet the family was

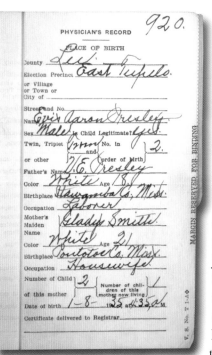

ABOVE: Elvis's birth certificate.
Topham Picturepoint 0529918

incredibly close-knit, with Gladys noticeably over-protective of her surviving son; she would reportedly attempt to walk him to school well into his teens.

The congregation of the Pentecostal First Assembly of God would be Elvis Presley's first audience. He loved to hear the choir and would later recall how he'd "slip off my mother's lap and stand there singing along." He didn't know the words but "I could carry a tune…the church gave me the only singing training I ever had. All the rest came naturally."

The activities of the preachers also entertained the young Elvis as they delivered their fire and brimstone sermons. "They cut up all over the place, moving every which way, sometimes jumping on the piano." Perhaps the black-influenced style of psalm singing wasn't the only thing he picked up on his Sunday excursions to church…and it's ironic that his own on-stage antics would later incur the wrath of the religious community.

Elvis moved with his parents to Maple Street in East Tupelo in 1940, then to Berry Street five years later. Several more changes of location followed, with Vernon apparently trying to keep one step ahead of his creditors. So impoverished were the Presleys, in fact, that all the family's

Elvis with his mother, Gladys, and father, Vernon, in 1937. *Michael Ochs Archives/Corbis 42-17536516*

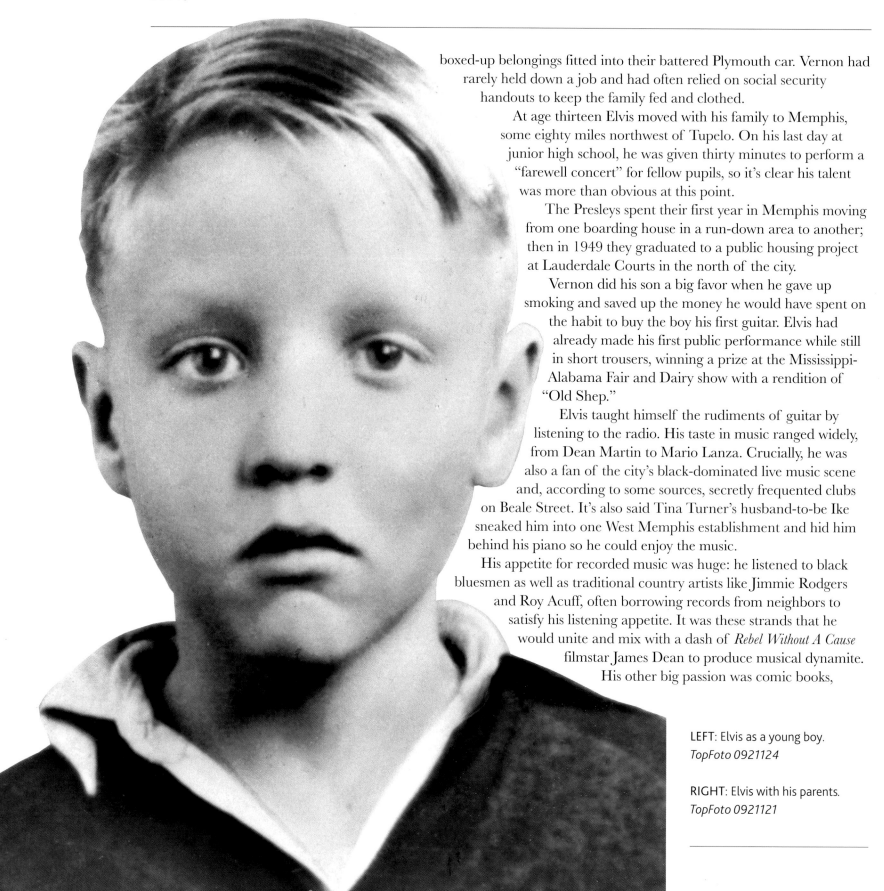

boxed-up belongings fitted into their battered Plymouth car. Vernon had rarely held down a job and had often relied on social security handouts to keep the family fed and clothed.

At age thirteen Elvis moved with his family to Memphis, some eighty miles northwest of Tupelo. On his last day at junior high school, he was given thirty minutes to perform a "farewell concert" for fellow pupils, so it's clear his talent was more than obvious at this point.

The Presleys spent their first year in Memphis moving from one boarding house in a run-down area to another; then in 1949 they graduated to a public housing project at Lauderdale Courts in the north of the city.

Vernon did his son a big favor when he gave up smoking and saved up the money he would have spent on the habit to buy the boy his first guitar. Elvis had already made his first public performance while still in short trousers, winning a prize at the Mississippi-Alabama Fair and Dairy show with a rendition of "Old Shep."

Elvis taught himself the rudiments of guitar by listening to the radio. His taste in music ranged widely, from Dean Martin to Mario Lanza. Crucially, he was also a fan of the city's black-dominated live music scene and, according to some sources, secretly frequented clubs on Beale Street. It's also said Tina Turner's husband-to-be Ike sneaked him into one West Memphis establishment and hid him behind his piano so he could enjoy the music.

His appetite for recorded music was huge: he listened to black bluesmen as well as traditional country artists like Jimmie Rodgers and Roy Acuff, often borrowing records from neighbors to satisfy his listening appetite. It was these strands that he would unite and mix with a dash of *Rebel Without A Cause* filmstar James Dean to produce musical dynamite. His other big passion was comic books,

LEFT: Elvis as a young boy.
TopFoto 0921124

RIGHT: Elvis with his parents.
TopFoto 0921121

which he devoured with the same passion he gave to his musical activities.

Elvis enrolled in LC Humes High School where he earned a reputation by letting his hair grow, not to mention a penchant for wearing brightly colored jackets over the school's regulation black trousers. Things were going well for the Presley family, who moved out of the housing project as they were earning more than the permitted maximum. They did, however, decide to stay in the neighborhood where they had finally put down roots.

Presley graduated from high school in 1953, marking the event by appearing in Humes' annual Minstrel Show and bringing the house down with a rendition of Teresa Brewer's recent hit "Till I Waltz Again With You." "It was amazing how popular I became after that," he'd later reflect with a grin. His attraction to the opposite sex was undoubted: his first girlfriend was Magdaline Morgan, the pair enjoying an innocent relationship when both were just thirteen.

He went to work first at a local machinists' shop, going on to become a delivery driver for an electrical store—a job that paid the future King of Rock 'n' Roll a princely $35 a week. It was while driving his truck that Presley paid an off-duty visit to Sun Records' Memphis Recording Services studios that summer to avail himself of a four-dollar "record yourself" offer.

He planned to cut a one-off disc for mother Gladys's birthday, and accompanied himself on guitar singing the 1948 pop hit "My Happiness" and the Ink Spots' "That's Where Your Heartaches Begin." Sam Phillips thought the boy had something: the rest is history.

"Elvis was the king. No doubt about it. People like myself, Mick Jagger and all the others only followed in his footsteps."
~ Rod Stewart

Elvis with his parents. *TopFoto 0921132*

Elvis holds a stack of "That's All Right (Mama)" his first commercial recording, 1954. *Bettmann/Corbis BE083926*

Chapter 2

Sam Phillips and Sun

"Rock 'n' roll music, if you like it, if you feel it, you can't help but move to it. That's what happens to me. I can't help it." ~ **Elvis Presley**

LEFT: The famous Sun Studio in Memphis where Elvis Presley made his first recording.
John Van Hasselt/Corbis

SAM PHILLIPS AND SUN

"It all came out of that infectious beat and those young people wanting to feel good by listening to some records."
~ Sam Phillips

The Sun Studios at 706 Union Avenue, Memphis, Tennessee, was, quite simply, the birthplace of Rock 'n' Roll. When Elvis Presley first passed through the doors one saturday in the summer of 1953 to take advantage of that offer as a present for his mother, it didn't just signal the beginning of the Sun Records success story—it began a teen revolution.

Further greats like Jerry Lee Lewis, Carl Perkins, and Johnny Cash would follow Presley into the studio and begin careers that would shape the foundations of modern music. But Elvis was first and foremost.

At the head of the operation was former radio announcer Sam Phillips, who founded the Sun label and led it through its most successful period from its inception in 1952 until he sold it in 1969. While hyperbolic terms like "revolutionary" and "visionary" are all too often used, it is safe to say it was Phillips's passion and perception that enabled Sun to create music history.

Sam Phillips was born in 1923, in Florence, Alabama and became the man who opened the door through which Rock 'n' Roll swaggered onto the world stage. In 1873, fifty years earlier, Florence, Alabama had been the birthplace of W.C. Handy, the man who opened the door through which the

ABOVE AND RIGHT: Sun Studios, Memphis. *John Coletti/JAI/Corbis 42-23731016 and John Van Hasselt/Corbis 42-20938535*

Blues had elbowed its way onto the world stage. So, in the span of half a century, Florence, Alabama had produced two visionaries who revolutionized twentieth century music.

After a career in law was derailed due to financial restraints, Phillips made the decision to follow his interest in radio, studying audio engineering at university. He appeared on various radio stations in his native Alabama and Nashville, Tennessee, before settling at WREC in Memphis. He was the right man in the right place at the right time.

He would originally launch Memphis Recording Service on the Union Avenue site; he recorded any event or occasion and sold the results to the participants. He remembered: "I had to do everything I possibly could do to get those doors open—I wasn't going to turn anything down. I just about did anything as long as it was half-way legal!"

After an ill-fated attempt at a self-titled record company, Phillips began recording artists through MRS, leasing the recordings to larger labels to release. "Rocket 88," performed by Jackie Brenston and Ike Turner, was the most successful of these. It topped the R&B chart in 1951 when leased to the Chess Records and its success convinced Phillips this was his calling. "In the sense of the term Rock 'n' Roll—which to me wrapped up black and white youth and vitality—it really was the first Rock 'n' Roll record."

A fall-out at WREC saw Phillips commit to his company full-time that same year before his second attempt at a record label saw Sun created in February 1952.

Memphis Recording Service's motto had been "We record anything, anywhere—any time," and it proved to be true as Sun welcomed any budding musician from Memphis and elsewhere; the diverse musical scene in the Tennessee city ensured an eclectic pool of talent. The raw, primeval sounds they left behind would prove inspirational to generations to come. By 1954 Phillips had upgraded his equipment and installed two Ampex 350 recorders, the second providing the essential tape delay echo or slapback that gave the Sun sound such a vibrant, three-dimensional quality.

The 1950s was a decade where racial division remained at the forefront of American society. But Phillips was not concerned; Sun originally specialized in electric blues recordings from black artists. "There is no greater thing to do than the blues if you are a musician," Phillips would later say. "There is nothing easier or more difficult. It's a symphony of the soul, there is no question about it."

But these black artists who got their break at Sun were so rapidly successful that they moved on to labels that could distribute them to a larger audience. Blues singer Howlin' Wolf, for instance, auditioned for Sun in 1951, but migrated to Chess Records the same year.

Phillips wanted a sound that was distinctively Sun, and wanted to discover the act that could make him his million by finding a "white man that sung black." "I'd been looking for a person, white-skinned, that could put the feel of a black person into a phonograph record." Enter a teenager named Elvis Aaron Presley.

Initially unimpressive, Presley sang ballads, but Phillips stuck with him and one night, during a session with guitarist Scotty Moore and bassist Bill Black, Presley repaid his patience, delivering a performance of "That's All Right (Mama)" that would make him a superstar.

ABOVE: The famous Sun Studio is a museum today. *John Van Hasselt/Corbis 42-20938534*

Four more singles would be released on Sun, but when the calculating Colonel Tom Parker, who already looked after country star Hank Snow, became Presley's manager, Elvis's time at Sun was ticking away. His contract with sold on to RCA in late 1955 for $40,000—a large amount of money for a struggling concern such as Sam's.

Phillips and Parker had taken an instant dislike to one another and the deal was acrimonious. The Colonel told Sam that Sun Records was too small an operation to handle an artist with as much potential as Elvis, adding that he should be signed to a record company with worldwide distribution. Sam knew Sun could only take Elvis so far, but the Colonel's abrasive personality raised his hackles.

It was inevitable that two such strong personalities would clash. Sam's drive to create original music was matched by the Colonel's drive to make money. But Sam was also a shrewd businessman who saw Presley's money-making potential. He kept his mouth shut and let the Colonel have his head. There was nothing he could do to stop him.

The Colonel, meanwhile, had been to see Elvis's parents, seducing them with talk of mass exposure, worldwide record deals, television appearances, and movie stardom. With Vernon and Gladys Presley onside, Parker called Phillips and offered to buy Elvis's contract. Sam, bowing to the inevitable, asked for $40,000 ($35,000, plus $5,000 he owed Elvis in back royalties).

The Colonel balked at the deal but Sam stood firm. The Colonel put together a consortium that included RCA Records ($25,000 plus Elvis's back royalties was as high as they would go), Hill & Range music publishers (who came up with $5,000), and the Colonel himself (who put in $5,000 of his own money). On November 21, 1955, all the principals gathered in Sun Studios to sign the deal and Elvis Presley became an RCA Victor recording artist.

When the deal was signed and sealed, Sam took Elvis aside and gave him some parting advice. "Stand on your own," he said. "Don't let them tell you what to do. You know how to do it now, so do it your own way."

The then considerable "transfer fee" ensured the cash-strapped Sun's survival to nurture the likes of Roy Orbison, Johnny Cash, and Jerry Lee Lewis, even if the jewel in the crown had gone elsewhere. With the money that was left, he formed a partnership with a friend and went into the hotel business. They built a hotel which was so successful they built a second. Then a third. They called them Holiday Inns.

With the focus of the music industry switching to LPs in the 1960s, Sun's forte of cutting classic singles was no longer cutting-edge—even though that vibrant yellow label on a seven-inch piece of black plastic remains today as iconic as anything in rock history. With those facts in mind, and with Sun's back catalogue commanding a high price, Phillips sold the company to former Mercury Records executive Shelby Singleton in 1969.

Under the leadership of Sam Phillips, Sun Records had an incredible run, launching some of the world's biggest and best artists from the 18-foot by 33-foot studio in Memphis. That tiny room was a positive for Phillips, as he said: "I didn't ever feel that I was being cheated by not having some of the set-ups I'd seen even then. Doing what we did with what we had certainly did not hinder us. It could have been responsible for some of the original feel that we got."

Guitarist Scotty Moore also paid tribute to the studio. "The sound, even with the gear they have in there now, is

ABOVE: Sam Phillips. *Michael Ochs Archives/Getty Images 74290370*

still special. It has to do with that old asbestos square acoustic tile, which covers everything but the floor. When you speak, you can feel the air pressure in the room. The more volume that you put into that room, the more the midrange compresses."

Technology has advanced immeasurably since those early pioneering days, of course. But it speaks volumes that, when supergroup U2 filmed their US tour in the late 1980s (it emerged as the album/movie package *Rattle And Hum*), they were insistent on coming to Memphis and using the same facilities, even down to the vocal microphone their heroes had used.

Chapter 3

The Sun Rises

"The first time that I appeared on stage, it scared me to death. I really didn't know what all the yelling was about. I didn't realize that my body was moving. It's a natural thing to me. So to the manager backstage I said, 'What'd I do? What'd I do?' And he said 'Whatever it is, go back and do it again'." ~ Elvis Presley from *Elvis on Tour*

LEFT: Today Elvis's statue stands in front of the Municipal Auditorium on 705 Elvis Presley Blvd., Shreveport. The statue next to him is of guitarist James Burton who played on the staff band at the Hayride and would perform with Elvis at Vegas in the 1960s. *Richard T. Nowitz/Corbis ulls046675*

THE SUN RISES

"This boy had everything. He had the looks, the moves, the manager, and the talent. And he didn't look like Mr. Ed like a lot of the rest of us did. In the way he looked, way he talked, way he acted... he really was different." ~ Carl Perkins

When Elvis walked into the Sun studio in 1953 to record "My Happiness" and an abortive version of the Ink Spots' "That's When Your Heartaches Begin" which stopped abruptly, Sam Phillips was intrigued. After the singer had left, he wrote in the studio log: "Good ballad singer. Hold." Presley went back to his job in Crown Electrics and waited for a call back. But nothing happened so he went back into Sun to privately record two more songs. Six months later, when the call finally came, Elvis was in the studio almost before the receptionist had put the phone down.

On this occasion, Phillips got Presley to sing just about every song that he knew. His favorite artists were the Ink Spots and Dean Martin, so the songs were mainly ballads. After three hours, Sam called it a day. The results were inconclusive. There had been no "Eureka!" moment, but Sam thought it worth going a little further.

He phoned local guitarist Scotty Moore and asked him to put Elvis through his paces. A meeting was set up at Scotty's house, along with bass-player Bill Black. They

ABOVE: "That's All Right (Mama)" was Elvis's first single. *GAB Archive/Redferns/ Getty Images 85224234*

spent an afternoon going through Elvis's repertoire. When Elvis left, Moore phoned Sam with his verdict. He wasn't overly impressed but admitted "The kid can sing." Phillips suggested they try again, this time at the studio with Bill Black.

The following night, they gathered at the studio. They wouldn't have realized it at the time but all the elements were already in place. All they lacked was the magic song. They spent the evening trying out different songs, still mainly ballads, but nothing clicked. Presley got more and more frustrated, thinking his chance was slipping away.

Consumed by a sense of desperation, he began changing vocal lines and lyrics, searching for something that had never been done before. Still nothing clicked. From the control booth, Sam told them to take a break. It was getting late and there was talk about calling it a day. During the break Elvis suddenly started singing "That's All Right (Mama)," an old blues number by Arthur "Big Boy" Crudup. Scotty and Bill joined in. This wasn't serious. This was just a bit of fun.

In the control room, Sam froze. This was what he'd been looking for. A white man who could sing black. He

Judy Tyler, Bill (bass), Elvis, and Scotty (guitar) in the recording studio for *Jailhouse Rock. John Springer Collection/Corbis JS1567844*

Within the image: FEBRUARY'S BIGGEST HI FI BUY... ARTUR RUBINSTEIN ON RCA VICTOR $2.98

THE SABRES RCA VICTOR

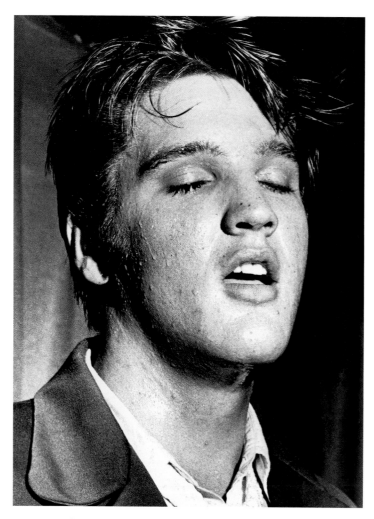

over the top, Elvis's uninhibited voice soared into uncharted territory. Sam knew they were getting close, so he started recording. A couple of takes later the song was in the can. None of them knew what they'd done. But one thing was for sure—it was certainly different. They'd just invented Rockabilly.

Sam Phillips had found what he was looking for but, having found it, didn't know what to do with it. He needed a second opinion and, later that night he got it. His old friend, Dewey Phillips, a Memphis disc-jockey on WHBQ radio, called in at Sun Studios in the early hours after his radio show. This was not unusual. Dewey, one of the few white DJs in the south who occasionally played black music, needed to wind down and there was no better way to do it than have a few beers and talk music with Sam.

Sam played him "That's All Right (Mama)." Dewey didn't know what to make of the song at first but, after repeated plays, fell in love with it. He promised to give it a spin on his show the following night, so Sam ran off an acetate for him. The next morning, Sam called Elvis to tell him he was going to be on the radio that night. As the time approached, Elvis, consumed by nerves, tuned the family radio to WHBQ so his parents could listen.

Half-an-hour into the show, Dewey played "That's All Right (Mama)" and the WHBQ switchboard lit up. Forty-seven calls came in, each wanting to hear the song again. Dewey phoned the Presley home to get Elvis over to the station for an interview, but was stunned to find out that he had gone to the movies. The Presleys went down to the theater, found him and sent him off to the radio station.

On arrival, Elvis was shaking with nerves. Sensing this, Dewey pretended to cue up a couple of records and started chatting to him, leaving the microphone open. During the conversation he asked him what school he had gone to. "Humes High School," came the reply. Dewey made sure he got that in because, in the educationally segregated south, that told listeners that he was white. At the end of the interview, Dewey thanked Elvis and played "That's All Right (Mama)" again.

"Aren't you gonna interview me?" asked Elvis. "Just did," said Dewey.

was surprised that Elvis even knew the song, so different was it from the ballads that had gone before. Keeping his voice level, he told them to work out a beginning and an end so they could record it. Elvis, Scotty and Bill were surprised. They'd only been fooling around, but they did as they were told. They worked on the arrangement, guided by Sam, and stripped the song down to its basics.

Scotty, like many guitarists of the day, was a devotee of Chet Atkins, the doyen of country pickers. Sam told him to cut back on the Atkins style and find his own way through the song. Without a drummer, Bill's bass had to drive the song. Using a slap technique, he set up a fearsome, hypnotic rhythm that, along with Elvis's acoustic guitar, perfectly complemented Scotty's pared-back guitar. And

During the show there had been upwards of 500 calls, and by the time the record was cut and released there were already advance orders for twelve times as many copies. Sam sent promotional copies out to all the local radio stations who began featuring it heavily.

Elvis, Scotty, and Bill started playing live shows. Scotty and Bill were seasoned musicians and took it in their stride but Elvis was paralysed with nerves. The debut gig, a guest spot at the Bon Air Club, a Memphis drinking club that featured hillbilly music, was a disaster, but first-night nerves had disappeared when they opened for Slim Whitman at Overton Park on the outskirts of Memphis.

During the first number, Elvis's leg began to shake uncontrollably and a frisson of excitement ran through the female members of the audience. During the second number they started to scream, and the more he shook, the more they screamed. Pandemonium reigned. Sam Phillips, watching in the wings, was astonished. Everybody was astonished. Even Slim Whitman mentioned Elvis during his set, saying that the boy was a hard act to follow.

Excitement grew exponentially among fans—helped immensely by the band's weekly slot on the Louisiana Hayride radio show. His first Hayride appearance came in October 1954 singing both sides of his debut single, and his last in December 1955, a benefit for the YMCA. In between came a regional television debut on the show in March 1955. Some traditional country fans were outraged by his antics, but it was clear that when it came to live performance this boy was in a league of his own.

One of those who witnessed Presley in his early performing period was Roy Orbison, then a would-be songwriter. The Big O would soon follow in Elvis's footsteps and knock on Sam Phillips's door, but what he saw in 1954 was positively inspirational. "It was at the Big D Jamboree in Dallas and the first thing, he came out and spit on the stage…it affected me exactly the same way as when I first saw that David Lynch film. There was just no reference point in the culture to compare it to." In short, Orbison concluded, "He was the firstest with the mostest."

The five singles Elvis Presley recorded for Sun will go down in history. All followed the same blueprint; country song one side, R&B the other, all backed by Moore's fine rockabilly guitar and Black's slapped bass. There's no doubt that these ten songs changed the course of popular music. For further details, consult the track notes that accompany this book's companion CD.

The last word should, perhaps, be left with Scotty Moore, one of the handful of men who shared the King's Sun rise. Elvis, he said, "had a feel for rhythm in his voice. He could hear a song and he knew what he could do with a song. And nobody else could do it."

LEFT: *Corbis IH014687*

BELOW: Elvis backstage on *The Ed Sullivan Show* while members of his band rehearse behind him, September 9, 1956. *CBS Photo Archive/Getty Images 76857899*

THE LOUISIANA HAYRIDE

On Saturday, October 16, 1954, Elvis sang for the first time on the Louisiana Hayride, a live country music radio show from Shreveport, Louisiana, broadcast by KWKH Radio. The first show didn't set the world on fire, although the second—in front of a younger audience—was good enough for him to be offered a one-year contract which he signed on November 2, 1954. He agreed to appear on the Hayride every Saturday night for the contracted year for $18.00 a performance (Scotty and Bill got $12.00 each). The Hayride helped Elvis's early rise to stardom, and in October 1955 the contract was renewed for another year—with an improved remuneration of $200 a show. However, it became increasingly difficult for Elvis to make it back to Shreveport every weekend, particularly when he signed up for his first movie. Colonel Tom Parker, by then Elvis's manager, bought him out of the contract and his last regular weekly appearance was on March 31, 1956. The buy-out cost $10,000 and the promise to appear on the special Hayride charity show on December 15, 1956 at the Hirsch Youth Center, after which Horace Logan told the audience "Elvis has left the building," coining a new phrase.

LEFT AND RIGHT: Elvis and the band at the Hayride of January 1, 1955. Sunset *Boulevard/Corbis 0000294483-007 and 0000294483-008*

BELOW: Elvis Presley's Martin D-18 serial #80221 dates back to January 15, 1942, when it was made at Martin's factory in Nazareth, PA. Elvis traded his Martin 000-18 for the D-18 at O.K. Houck Piano Co. in Memphis in late 1954 . The stick-on letters came with the guitar when he bought it at Houck's. Elvis changed it for a 1955 Martin D-28 with a leather-tooled cover that can be seen at right. On loan to the Country Music Hall of Fame 1974–1991 it was sold to a British collector, who sold it to Michael Malone for $151,700 in 1993. *Getty Images 103151733*

Chapter 4

Elvis's Band—Scotty, Bill and DJ

"It was Scotty Moore's guitar riff when he was doing the Steve Allen Show that got me into rock music. I've been an Elvis fan since I was a kid." ~ **Elton John**

LEFT: Elvis Presley and his band on stage. *Bettmann/Corbis ulls046675*

ELVIS'S BAND—SCOTTY, BILL AND DJ

"When I first heard Elvis' voice I just knew that I wasn't going to work for anybody; and nobody was going to be my boss. Hearing him for the first time was like busting out of jail." ~ Bob Dylan

When Elvis Presley walked into the Sun studios in July 1954 to cut his first single, guitarist Scotty Moore was by his side. Moore's rockabilly licks, played on a semi-acoustic Gibson ES-295, added instrumental excitement to the likes of "That's All Right (Mama)," "Good Rockin' Tonight," and "Mystery Train."

Winfield Scott Moore was born on December 27, 1931, in Gadsden, Tennessee. He started playing guitar at the age of eight. At sixteen, but claiming to be eighteen, he joined the U.S. Navy and served four years on the aircraft carrier USS *Valley Forge*. He took his guitar with him. On his discharge, he returned to Tennessee, settling in Memphis. He formed the Starlite Wranglers, a hillbilly band, and formed a close friendship with bass-player Bill Black. Scotty, self-possessed and shrewd, began to manage the band and they became well-known in the Memphis area, his fleet-fingered guitar style the main selling point.

The obvious next step was to make a record, so Scotty went to see Sam Phillips at Sun Records on Union Avenue. Sam had heard of them and agreed to a studio date, so the Wranglers went in and recorded two songs (you've got to have a B-side). Sun released a single but it only sold 245 copies. That seemed the end of that. But Sam was sitting on a time bomb.

Sam and Scotty were kindred spirits. Both were ambitious and both were searching for something different. When Sam encountered Elvis, he arranged for Scotty to put him through his paces. A meeting was set up at Scotty's house, along with Bill Black, the Wranglers' bass-player. They spent an afternoon going through Elvis's repertoire, all ballads. When Elvis left, Scotty phoned up Sam with his verdict. He wasn't overly impressed, but admitted, "The kid can sing." Sam suggested they try again, this time at the studio. Scotty asked if he should bring the Starlite Wranglers along. "No," said Sam, "just Bill."

William Patton Black was born in Memphis on September 17, 1926, one of nine children. He shared the same poor upbringing as Elvis, and at one time lived in the same Lauderdale Court apartment complex; indeed, it's said their mothers were friends.

His first instrument was a home-made bass fashioned by his father by nailing together a cigar box and a plank and attaching strings. Two years later, age sixteen, he was playing hillbilly songs on guitar in a local bar. His future wife Evelyn, whom he met while on war service, was also a guitarist, and they married in 1946.

He linked with Scotty Moore in 1952, having meanwhile mastered the full-size upright bass, and the

Elvis and Scotty in concert, 1956. *Michael Ochs Archives/Corbis 42-17536515*

Elvis and the band play for his hometown crowd September 27, 1956. *Bettmann/Corbis BE031625*

combination of the laconic guitarist and fun-loving, clowning bass player proved a winning one.

The Starlite Wranglers session may have been a failure but Sam Phillips had been impressed by Scotty, in whom he sensed a kindred spirit. Both were ambitious and both were searching for something different. So when Sam needed to find out Elvis's musical range, who better to do it than Scotty? The guitarist, for his part, was delighted. Sam's secretary, Marion Keisker, had suggested Elvis as someone Scotty could work with and he'd been pestering Sam for his phone number.

As has been mentioned already, Elvis went to Scotty's house on Sunday, July 4, 1954. Scotty had arranged for Bill Black to be there and the two of them auditioned Elvis. As Scotty tells in his autobiography, *That's All Right Elvis*, Bill wasn't impressed but Scotty still recommended Elvis to Phillips and the next day they went to Sun Records for the first, momentous recording session.

Scotty always gave Elvis the main share of credit for what happened, praising his "sense of rhythm" and "great vocal control"—but he also shared the praise around, suggesting that Bill Black with his uptempo bass slapping also contributed a great deal. Bill acted as MC when the band played live and was very charismatic. Scotty, as an old studio hand, was able to add a great deal of counterpoint to Elvis' singing style—and a winning team was the result.

In October 1954 the trio of Elvis, Scotty, and Bill were joined by drummer Dominic Joseph Fontana, born March 15, 1931, in Shreveport, Louisiana. Known universally as DJ, he completed an outfit sometimes billed as the Blue Moon Boys, and would enjoy a fifteen-year association with the King. Prior to this he had been employed by the Louisiana Hayride to be an in-house drummer on its Saturday night radio broadcast. This is where Elvis first encountered him, though Fontana played from behind a curtain as purist country fans did not like drums. Fontana has stated he did not play on Elvis's later Sun recordings, this honor having apparently fallen to one Johnny Bernero.

When Elvis went into RCA's Nashville Studios on January 10, 1956, two days after he officially entered adulthood. Black, Moore, and Fontana were there with

ABOVE: Elvis with Scotty Moore behind, June 22, 1956.
Bettmann/Corbis BE065157

him, alongside session-men, Floyd Cramer on piano and guitarist Chet Atkins, a star in his own right. Presley was unfazed and laid down the charged melancholia of "Heartbreak Hotel," which became his first Number 1, and several tracks for his self-titled first album.

When Elvis entered the Army in 1958 the madness that had consumed the lives of Scotty, Bill, and DJ for the previous two years suddenly stopped. It's quite possible there was a sense of relief. In spite of the millions that were swelling the Presley coffers, Bill and DJ were paid a derisory $200 a week. In the early days, they'd split the gig money equally, Elvis getting the same as everybody else but the Colonel put the band on wages. Scotty walked out but, after Hank "Sugarfoot" Garland stood in for the next few gigs, Elvis rang him up and begged him to come back. It can be assumed an improved wage was part of the package. Bill, meanwhile, went off and joined a Memphis band which soon morphed into the Bill Black Combo. They developed a groove and stuck to it, and it earned them eight Top Forty hits, including "Smokie," which reached Number 17. Their muscular, sax-led instrumentals were great to dance to, and they became jukebox favorites, one of those bands whose influence goes way beyond their recorded output. Sadly, in 1965, at the age of just thirty-nine, Bill Black died from a brain tumor.

When Elvis came out of the army Scotty Moore was re-hired for the first sessions, which produced the *Elvis Is Back* album, and two singles, "It's Now Or Never" and "Are You Lonesome Tonight?". He

continued his studio work with Elvis for another four years before handing in his notice. During this time there were no live performances, giving Scotty time to pursue a parallel professional life. He went back to work for Sam Phillips at Sun as studio production manager. He also opened his own studio and started up his own Belle Meade label.

The last time Scotty worked with Elvis was on the NBC-TV's 1968 Comeback Special. The concept, unusually engineered by Presley rather than Colonel Parker, was for Elvis to sing his Rock 'n' Roll songs accompanied by Scotty Moore and DJ Fontana and interspersed with banter about the old days.

They sat in a tight circle, face to face with Elvis. Scotty sat to his immediate left playing his blonde Gibson electric and DJ sat directly in front of him, playing on an empty guitar case. They kicked off with "That's All Right (Mama)." It sounded a little ragged but the old magic was still there.

Scotty was offered a place in Elvis's Las Vegas band but declined. His replacement was James Burton—not a bad second choice. Moore and Fontana have since performed together with others, including a 2002 recording of "That's All Right (Mama)" with Paul McCartney. In 1983 the drummer published a book titled *DJ Fontana Remembers Elvis*.

LEFT: A 1952 Gibson ES-295—one of only 1,770 built. Scotty used a guitar like this on the Sun Sessions. *Nigel Osbourne/Redferns/Getty Images 102169478*

RIGHT: L–R: Elvis, Bill, Scotty, and Sam Philips in the Sun Records studio. *GAB Archive/Redferns/Getty Images 85362102*

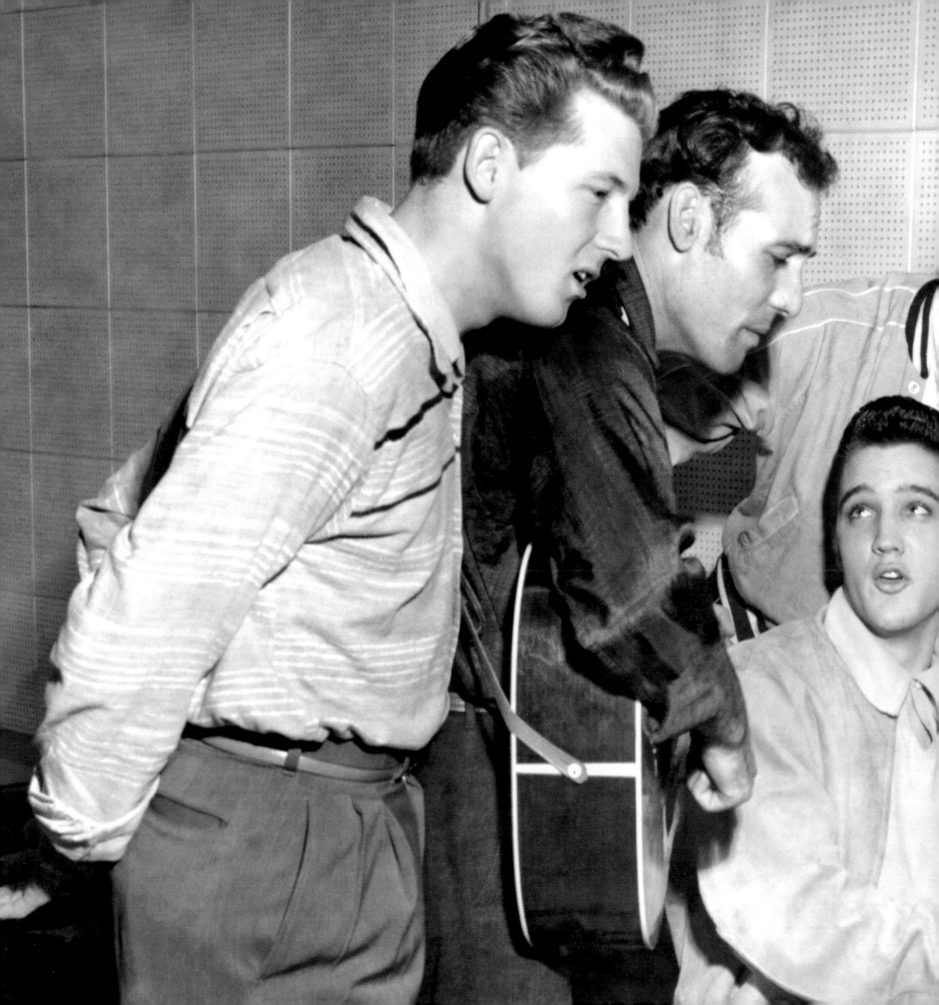

Chapter 5

The Million Dollar Quartet

"It was what you might call a barrelhouse of fun. Carl Perkins was in a recording session...
  "Johnny Cash dropped in. Jerry Lee Lewis was there too, and then I stopped by..." **~ Elvis Presley**

LEFT: The Million Dollar Quartet was really an impromptu jam on December 4, 1956, between four famous musicians recorded by Sam Phillips at his Sun Studios. L–R: Jerry Lee Lewis, Carl Perkins, Elvis, Johnny Cash. *Michael Ochs Archives/Corbis 42-17536519*

THE MILLION DOLLAR QUARTET

"I never had a better time than yesterday afternoon when I dropped into Sam Phillips' place." ~ Elvis Presley

The fourth day of December 1956 saw Elvis return to Sun to play music with three friends. They did so in a relaxed—and what they thought was an unrecorded—environment. What happened that day, the coming together of four legends of Rock 'n' Roll in the place of its birth, Sun Records' studio in Memphis, became known as the Million Dollar Quartet sessions.

Carl Perkins was recording in the studio that afternoon. Promotion of his single, "Blue Suede Shoes," had been halted by a serious car crash, so he had come back with new material, aiming to emulate his earlier success. Also taking part in the recording was pianist Jerry Lee Lewis, who had recently signed to Sun and had a single ready to release.

Jerry Lee was assisting Perkins on his new material at the request of Sam Phillips, who wanted to add a new dimension to Perkins' sound. Being a young artist, Lewis was strapped for cash and, with Christmas fast approaching, was happy to lend a hand.

As the session drew to a close, Elvis arrived to see his old friend Carl, whom he had grown close to after they had played the bars of the mid-South trying to establish themselves.

Lewis remembers the day, but prefers to think he was the center of attention: "I'd never met Elvis at the time; he had just got back from Florida, and I was (in Memphis), and he called me to see if I was (in Memphis), as he wanted to meet me. So he came and parked up right in front of Sun Records, in a white Lincoln Continental Mark II. He came in, we met, and he sat down next to the piano. We started singing, playing. Every time Johnny or Carl would try singing or doing something, Elvis would start singing!"

Sun Records had been the launch-pad for Presley's career but it had been a year since label founder Phillips had sold Presley's contract to RCA Victor to ease crippling debts.

However, there were no hard feelings; Presley had begun to achieve world fame with the backing of a major label, while Phillips knew he had other irons in the fire— namely Perkins and a young musician by the name of Johnny Cash. Cash had signed for Sun the same time as Perkins and, while perhaps not as suited for uptempo Rock 'n' Roll, had written his name in the charts earlier in the year with the classic "I Walk The Line."

Debate has raged among rockabilly enthusiasts as to whether Cash was present for the whole session or not, due to his voice not being picked up clearly on the tapes. Rumor has it that Phillips recognized the importance of what he was witnessing and, sensing a photo opportunity, summoned him some way into proceedings. However Cash himself denies this and claims he was present from the off, stating he was singing in a different key in order to keep up with Presley.

The four boys started singing an array of gospel songs, in deference to their roots, before playing several rockier numbers. Most of these were covers of previously released tracks that had influenced them, though they also showcased their own songs. There was plenty of banter between the four musicians, and even a moment when Presley talked about seeing Jackie Wilson (who he referred to as one of Billy Ward's Dominoes) in Vegas impersonating him—he then proceeded to imitate Wilson imitating him!

With four world-class talents under his roof, Phillips knew he had something. He called Bob Johnson, entertainment editor for the local newspaper—the *Memphis Press Scimitar*—who brought a photographer to capture the moment. All four performers were in shot, leaving the issue of Johnny Cash's involvement open. The next day Johnson coined the "Million-Dollar Quartet" phrase in his headline.

In an unrelated interview the following day Presley gave an insight to the jam session and backed up Cash's claims that he was present from the beginning: "I never had a better time than yesterday at Sam Phillips' place. It was what you might call a barrelhouse of fun. Carl Perkins was in a recording session and he had one that's going to hit as hard as 'Blue Suede Shoes.' Johnny Cash dropped in. Jerry Lewis was there too, and then I stopped by."

Even though the tapes were left running to cover the event, it was not until Phillips sold Sun Records to Shelby Singleton in 1969 that they were rediscovered and shared with the world. We know what happened to Elvis, but what became of the other three individuals?

1958 saw Carl Perkins depart for Columbia (CBS) Records, but he was based at Sun for perhaps his best years. He passed away in 1998 aged 65. One of the bands he influenced heavily was the Beatles: they performed and recorded many of his songs in their early years, George Harrison a particular devotee.

Johnny Cash made the same move to Columbia, citing the desire to record gospel on the label. He proceeded to have hits like "Don't Take Your Guns To Town" and the country Number 1 smash "Ring Of Fire" that crossed over to the music mainstream. He continued to write, record,

and perform with increasing authority until his death in 2003, while a 2005 bio-pic *I Walk The Line* starring Joaquin Phoenix and Reese Witherspoon added further luster to the legend.

Jerry Lee Lewis rocketed into the charts with his first two hits for Sun, "Whole Lotta Shakin' Goin' On" and "Great Balls Of Fire." Despite initial reservations about its "risqué" nature, the latter peaked at Number 2 on the *Billboard* Hot 100, while also topping the U.S. country charts. But this promising start would not last, as 1958 saw him embroiled in scandal after it was revealed he was married to his second cousin—who was only thirteen years old. But after some difficult years, Lewis returned to popularity and is still considered one of Sun and Rock 'n' Roll's true greats.

BELOW:The price of fame: Elvis found himself in court on assault charges on October 19, 1956. The day before he had pulled into a Memphis gas station and attracted a crowd. Station manager Ed Hopper asked him to leave. The situation escalated and Hopper cuffed Elvis on the back of his head. "Hey, man, don't be messing up my hair." The ensuing scuffle saw Elvis black the eye of the hefty Hopper (left) and tussle with 6-foot 4-inch Aubrey Brown (beside him), who also came off second best. Witnesses backed up Elvis's version of events and he was acquitted with his two assailants fined. *Topfoto 0257123*

Chapter 6

Colonel Tom Parker

"You don't have to be nice to people you meet on the way up if you're not coming back down again." ~ Colonel Tom Parker

LEFT: Colonel Tom Parker's Walk of Fame star, a commemorative plaque set in the pavement in Palm Springs. *Corbis ulls046675*

COLONEL TOM PARKER

"Don't try to explain it, just sell it." ~ Colonel Tom Parker

Every successful artist needs a manager—and, as Elvis's popularity escalated, he discovered he was no exception.

Sam Phillips suggested Scotty Moore do the job, and for a brief period he did, although it usually went no further than organizing transport and picking up the gig money. But, it soon became obvious that Scotty couldn't manage Elvis and play in the band. So Bob Neal, a Memphis DJ and entrepreneur, took over the reins. He didn't last long, being edged out by an ex-carnival huckster called Colonel Tom Parker.

Parker was previously best known for "Colonel Parker's Dancing Chickens," a major attraction on the carnival circuit. The chickens, caged and docile, suddenly became animated, jumping up and down when country music was played. They had no choice. The floor of their cage was a steel hotplate which, when the Colonel turned it on, became a barbecue grill. They either danced or fried.

But the carnival circuit was too small for the Colonel and he had moved into country music, becoming Eddy Arnold's manager for a time before becoming Hank Snow's agent. He'd heard about Elvis and decided to take a look. He caught up with him at a Louisiana Hayride show. He was impressed, particularly by the screaming girls. He began to smell dollar bills. He made no move but did offer Elvis a down-the-bill spot on a Hank Snow show.

Things moved fast once he became Presley's manager. His horizons for his young charge were limitless, and he thought that with himself at the helm, Elvis could go national—so behind everybody's back he approached RCA and suggested they sign Elvis. RCA showed interest, so Parker approached Sam and asked him how much he wanted for Elvis's contract. Sam, an artist and visionary, hated Parker, a ruthless philistine, so he pulled an astronomical figure out of the air—$35,000.

It may not seem like much in this day and age, but at the time it would have been the largest deal ever paid for a single artist, including established stars. The Colonel put together a consortium, putting in $5,000 of his own money, and met the asking price. Elvis, who was loyal to Sam Phillips, wasn't too keen on the deal so the Colonel went to visit Elvis's parents and convinced them that, with him in charge, untold riches awaited their son. With them on board, it was only a matter of time before Elvis changed his mind and the deal was done.

Colonel Parker's plan, conceived during Presley's army service, was to turn Elvis into an all-round family entertainer because that—by his reasoning—was where the big money lay. The way to achieve this, he believed, was to make Elvis as anodyne as possible, knock off all the edges, nullify the sexual menace, and avoid any hint of controversy at all costs. In practice, this meant churning out an endless stream of unthreatening Hollywood movies. *Jailhouse Rock* was replaced by *Fun In Acapulco*.

On the Colonel's orders, Hill and Range, Presley's publishing company, vetted the songs he was offered, ensuring that his recorded output wouldn't offend even the most casual listener, and live performance wasn't even considered because it was an uncontrolled environment with too many unpredictables. Under the Colonel's iron regime, Elvis became a compliant puppet. No one quite knows why he allowed this to happen. Maybe the Colonel kept him permanently mesmerized (in a previous incarnation, the Colonel had been a carnival-show hypnotist).

If this strategy had been successful, the Colonel would have been vindicated, not least commercially. But it hadn't

LEFT: Colonel Tom Parker's card from 1974. Michael Ochs Archives/Getty Images 74289825

BELOW: Elvis and Colonel Tom Parker in 1956. *Michael Ochs Archives/Corbis 42-17536517*

Colonel Tom was always in the background, making sure he was part of anything involving Elvis. Here, on February 14, 1964, Elvis hands over the papers for the SS *Potomac*, former presidential yacht of President Franklin D. Roosevelt, to Danny Thomas of St. Jude Hospital in Memphis, Tennessee. *Bettmann/Corbis U1412937*

worked. People stopped going to see his movies, his record sales plummeted and he was universally regarded as an artist whose time had passed. The King of Rock 'n' Roll was in danger of becoming a has-been. But still the Colonel pursued the all-round entertainer dream.

That said, of course, linking movies with albums was a policy many have since followed. He was an expert on making films on low budgets with opportunities for a dozen songs to be performed. The soundtrack album that followed helped the film's impact and cost next to nothing. And, given the majority of arguments between Parker and Presley revolved round the singer's unwillingness to tour, sending movies worldwide was a good alternative.

In any case, the Colonel refused to let his charge tour outside America. There are several theories that try to explain this. Recent research has come up with a plausible hypothesis. The Colonel was Dutch by birth. But suddenly, in his twenties, he emigrated to America. Just before he left Holland, there was a murder in Breda, his home town, and the Colonel was implicated. To this day the murder remains unsolved. Could it be that the Colonel was afraid to return to European jurisdiction?

His real name, it appears, was Andreas Cornelis van Kuijk and, though he had spent a short time in the U.S. Army around 1930, his title of "colonel" was purely honorary, having been conferred in 1948 by former country singer turned Louisiana governor Jimmy Davis.

Ultimately what is real and what is smoke and mirrors is beside the point. It's certain that without Colonel Parker's guidance the Elvis Presley story would have been dramatically different. Of course, he took his cut as his protégé made money—estimates range from twenty-five to fifty percent of the gross. He wrote the textbook for marketing a Rock 'n' Roll star, and undoubtedly reaped the rewards.

According to Presley biographer Peter Guralnick, Presley and Parker "were like a married couple, who started out with great love, loyalty, respect which lasted for a considerable period of time, and went through a number of stages until, towards the end of Presley's life, they should have walked away. None of the rules of the relationship were operative any longer, yet neither had the courage to walk away." Parker nevertheless remained Presley's manager until the singer's death in 1977.

Colonel Tom Parker died twenty years later in Las Vegas. His death certificate listed his birthplace as Holland, but his citizenship as American. Whatever his shadowy background, his legend will live on within the music business as the first entertainment impresario to work in Rock 'n' Roll.

BELOW: Colonel Tom Parker seated (second right) in front of a banner heralding "Elvis Presley in another great Hal Wallis production." Wallis took Elvis to Hollywood and produced nine of his films (*Loving You, King Creole, GI Blues, Blue Hawaii, Girls! Girls! Girls!, Fun in Acapulco, Roustabout, Paradise Hawaiian Style*, and *Easy Come, Easy Go*). *Michael Ochs Archives/Getty Images 74289820*

Chapter 7

Signing with RCA and the First Big Hits

"I always wanted to be this tough James Dean type, but Elvis was bigger than religion in my life. When I heard 'Heartbreak Hotel' it was so great I couldn't speak, I didn't want to say anything against Elvis, not even in my mind." ~ John Lennon

LEFT: Elvis signs autographs for a group of fans during filming of *Love Me Tender*.
Bettmann/Corbis BE037013

SIGNING WITH RCA AND THE FIRST BIG HITS

"He was white, but he sang black. It wasn't socially acceptable for white kids to buy black records at the time. Elvis filled a void."
~ Chet Atkins

It was a case of "Nashville Calling" when Elvis, who'd only just turned twenty-one, walked into the RCA studios in January 1956 to cut his first long-player. A $40,000 "transfer fee" lay on his young shoulders, but it was soon apparent that it weighed remarkably lightly. He was in the company of friends—his group Bill Black (bass), DJ Fontana, (drums) and Scotty Moore (guitar)—but also had in tow the Jordanaires.

To be accurate, one Jordanaire, Gordon Stoker. He sang with Speer Family members Ben and Brock Speer, but would appear with his regular partners on future records. Pianist Floyd Cramer and Chet Atkins, the famed guitarist and RCA's man in Nashville, made up the numbers.

Elvis performed the songs in the confines of the studio just as he would in concert, a felt pick being used to muffle the sound of his acoustic guitar which otherwise would have been picked up by other microphones. An indication of

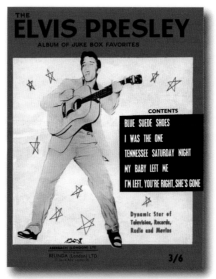

ABOVE: A book published in the UK, *The Elvis Presley album of juke box favorites* included "Blue Suede Shoes," "I Was The One," "Tennessee Saturday Night," "My Baby Left me," "I'm left, you're right, she's gone." *TopFoto 1067952*

how he must have looked comes from William Randolph's cover shot of Elvis strumming and singing on stage.

Gone was the intimacy of Sun Studios, replaced by the cavernous formality of a studio that produced music in industrial proportions. They were booked in for three three-hour sessions over two days. Steve Sholes sat in the producer's chair. He had no plan other than to get as close to the Sun sound as possible. When Elvis asked him what he had in mind, he shrugged his shoulders and said, "Just do what you usually do."

Sholes may have wanted to duplicate the Sun sound but didn't know how to get it. They tried various ways to achieve the "slapback" echo, but failed. That was Sam Phillips' secret. Sam's echo was a tape echo, but the closest the RCA engineers could get was to set up a microphone in a hallway and feed the effect back through the desk. It was a good, serviceable echo, but it wasn't slapback echo. They had no choice but to settle for it.

Elvis and Teddy Bears. "(Let Me Be Your) Teddy Bear" was written by Kal Mann and Bernie Lowe and became a U.S. Number 1 hit in summer 1957—the third of the four that he would have that year. *Michael Ochs Archives/Corbis 42-17853347*

While they were setting up, Scotty asked Chet Atkins what he had in mind. "Just do what you usually do," he replied. The only person who knew what to do was Elvis who, while listening to any advice offered, confidently followed his own star, seemingly oblivious to the jangling nerves around him.

Many of the songs were covers of well known artists such as Ray Charles, the Drifters, and Rodgers and Hart. Even the opening track—"Blue Suede Shoes"—was associated with its writer, Elvis's former Sun stablemate Carl Perkins. He had already taken the track to the U.S. Top Five, but, as luck would have it, he was hospitalized after a car crash on tour, leaving Elvis to register the hit elsewhere.

It's strange to think now but there was no guarantee RCA's investment would pay off. As Perkins' "Blue Suede Shoes" attacked the U.S. chart summit, Elvis's new label was having trouble getting "Heartbreak Hotel" off the ground. Sam Phillips was surprised to get a phone call from Sholes: "Be honest with me, Sam," said Sholes. "Did we sign the wrong man?" Time would render the question irrelevant; as "Heartbreak Hotel" rose to top the U.S. chart (it made Number 2 in Britain), it accounted for fifty percent of RCA's pop record sales.

BELOW AND RIGHT: Two views of Elvis on the set of *Love Me Tender* in August 1956: with Richard Egan and Debra Paget (below); and Mildred Dunnock and Paget (right). *Sunset Boulevard/Corbis 42-25492475 and 42-25492488*

The song, written by Mae Axton and Tommy Durden, wasn't an obvious choice for a single with lyrics that talked of broken-hearted lovers crying in the gloom, but Elvis had loved it when the writers had played it to him. "That's gonna be my first RCA single," he said. Cramer added a languid piano solo and, after a few takes, it was in the can.

It is almost impossible to overestimate the revolutionary nature of this track. Elvis's dramatic delivery drips with heartache, elevating what is essentially a blues into a gothic soundscape that seems to celebrate the tragic hopelessness of failed love. It was radically different to anything that had gone before. It didn't have the Sun Records sound, but it

had a mordant grace that was unique. Atkins, a quiet, self-contained country gentleman who probably had more experience of studio recording than any man alive, phoned his wife and told her to get down there as soon as she could. "You'll never see anything like this again," he told her. "It's so damn *exciting*."

He wasn't the only one to feel that way. Thousands of miles away across the Atlantic, the young John Lennon was listening. "When I first heard "Heartbreak Hotel" I could hardly make out what was being said," the Beatle to be would later recall. "It was just the experience of hearing it and having my hair stand on end. We'd never heard

American voices singing like that. They'd always sung like Sinatra who enunciated well. Suddenly, there's this hillbilly hiccupping with echo and all this bluesy background going on. We didn't know what the hell Presley was singing about or Little Richard or Chuck Berry. It took a long time to work out what was going on. To us, it just sounded like great noise."

ELVIS PRESLEY

RELEASED: March 23, 1956
RECORDED: July 1954–January 1956
LENGTH: 28:03
LABEL: RCA Victor

Side One
1. Blue Suede Shoes *Carl Perkins*
2. I'm Counting on You *Don Robertson*
3. I Got A Woman *Ray Charles and Renald Richard*
4. One-Sided Love Affair *Bill Campbell*
5. I Love You Because *Leon Payne*
6. Just Because *Sydney Robin, Bob Shelton, Joe Shelton*

Side Two
1. Tutti Frutti *Dorothy LaBostrie and Richard Penniman*
2. Trying to Get to You *Rose Marie McCoy and Margie Singleton*
3. I'm Gonna Sit Right Down and Cry (Over You) *Howard Biggs and Joe Thomas*
4. I'll Never Let You Go (Lil' Darlin') *Jimmy Wakely*
5. Blue Moon *Richard Rodgers and Lorenz Hart*
6. Money Honey *Jesse Stone*

The imaginatively titled *Elvis Presley* followed the single's lead to the top of the U.S. album chart in May with advance orders of 362,000, confirming this newcomer was no flash in the pan. Even younger listeners unfamiliar with the music will recognize the debut's cover as the inspiration for the Clash's *London Calling* (1979).

Interestingly, five of the LP's dozen tracks had been cut at Sun but were rejected by Sam Phillips. These included the ballads "Blue Moon," "I Love You Because," and "I'll Never Let You Go," songs his early mentor clearly felt did not fit the rebellious Presley image. Their inclusion makes the eventual release a more rounded offering that might otherwise have been the case. And with RCA's worldwide reach (British release happened via the HMV imprint), he was set to attract a global audience.

Second album *Elvis* took three days to cut, though this time the venue was Radio Recorders in Hollywood. There was a new pressure, since Elvis was now a potential matinee idol: indeed, shooting for his first film, *Love Me Tender*, had already begun. There are those who say Elvis's "Hollywood-ization" emasculated his music—if so, this was a blast of the wild, red-blooded rock star that used to be.

Unlike the first album, which had comprised five songs from the Sun studios and seven cut in Nashville, Elvis's thirteen tracks were all recorded of a piece. The same musicians employed previously were augmented by piano from the Jordanaires' Gordon Stoker—and, since Elvis had been annoyed by having to work with session men on music for his film debut, the assembled group had a point to prove.

Three tracks were borrowed from Little Richard's songbook—"Rip It Up," "Long Tall Sally," and "Ready Teddy," while Otis Blackwell, writer of the recent chart-topping single "Don't Be Cruel," contributed "Paralysed." The album did not include "Don't Be Cruel"/"Hound Dog," just as the debut had omitted the recent "Heartbreak Hotel"—but "Hound Dog" writers Leiber and Stoller came up with another winner in "Love Me," which would reach Number 2 when released as a single.

The track that most people remember on the album, however, was one on which Elvis himself played piano on

53

record for the first time. He'd performed "Old Shep" at a state fair at age ten and clearly still retained an affection for the song, even though it has since become his most lampooned track.

Elvis entered the U.S. charts at a then unprecedented Number 7 on the way to the summit, and by 1960 would

ELVIS

RELEASED: October 19, 1956
RECORDED: January and September 1956
LENGTH: 29:47
LABEL: RCA Victor
PRODUCER: Steve Sholes

Side One
1. Rip It Up *Robert Blackwell and John Marascalco*
2. Love Me *Jerry Leiber and Mike Stoller*
3. When My Blue Moon Turns to Gold Again *Gene Sullivan and Wiley Walker*
4. Long Tall Sally *Robert Blackwell, Enotris Johnson, Richard Penniman*
5. First in Line *Aaron Schroeder and Ben Weisman*
6. Paralyzed *Otis Blackwell and Elvis Presley*

Side Two
1. So Glad You're Mine *Arthur Crudup*
2. Old Shep *Red Foley*
3. Ready Teddy *Robert Blackwell and John Marascalco*
4. Anyplace Is Paradise *Joe Thomas*
5. How's the World Treating You? *Chet Atkins and Boudleaux Bryant*
6. How Do You Think I Feel *Webb Pierce and Wiley Walker*

be certified as having sold over three million copies. When Elvis Presley's impact on music is considered, it is usually measured in songs, often singles. But his first two albums, both recorded and released in 1956, still reverberate half a century later.

With two chart-topping albums to his credit in just seven short months, not to mention a slew of singles and EPs, the career of Elvis Aaron Presley was clearly progressing to manager Colonel Parker's complete satisfaction. It was a measure of Presley's success that when *Elvis' Golden Records* was released in April 1958, all fourteen of its tracks had been million-selling singles. There have been innumerable compilations since, but *Elvis' Golden Records* was the first and arguably greatest. The original album came complete with a flyer which, when returned by mail with 25 cents, would secure the purchaser an Elvis photo book.

Amazingly, *Elvis' Golden Records* peaked at a "mere" Number 3 in the U.S. charts—perhaps his fan base already owned the songs as singles—but would re-enter the Top 75 after his death nearly two decades later.

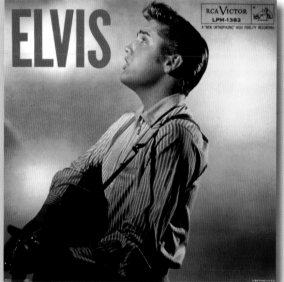

He'd followed up "Heartbreak Hotel" with further chart-toppers in "I Want You, I Need You, I Love You," "Don't Be Cruel," and "Hound Dog." The fourth and final U.S. Number 1 of the year was "Love Me Tender," the title song of his first movie that was adapted from the 19th century Civil War song "Aura Lee." It was very

ABOVE: *Elvis* was released in 1956 by RCA. *Michael Ochs Archive/Getty Images 85420355*

Elvis on the set of *King Creole*. *John Springer Collection/Corbis JS1564629*

nearly a hundred years old when Elvis tackled it.

The following year saw Elvis register four more Number 1 hits: "Too Much," "All Shook Up," "Teddy Bear," and "Jailhouse Rock," the latter another successful movie tie-in written by Jerry Leiber and Mike Stoller to title Presley's third movie. By the time this peaked in October 1957 Elvis had registered an impressive nine Number 1 U.S. singles.

Mind you, Britain wouldn't hear "Jailhouse Rock" until 1958, as the label's pressing plant was unable to meet then unheard-of advance orders of a quarter of a million! And while 1958 brought only two U.S. chart-topping singles, "Don't" and "Hard Headed Woman," six other hits ensured his name was constantly in the public eye.

Last—but far from least—a mention for "One Night" and "I Got Stung." Released as two sides of a late-1958 single, they both registered individually in the U.S. Top Ten. The disc would top Britain's chart in January 1959 as Elvis served Uncle Sam in Germany—the nearest, apart from an airport transfer, he would get to his UK fans. Its combination of frantic rock ("I Got Stung") and a bluesy updating of a 1956 Smiley Lewis hit ("One Night"), with suggestive lyrics toned down for radio play, showed how Tom Parker was intent on making Elvis all things to all fans.

By the time his fourth movie, *King Creole*, opened in July 1958 Elvis was a serving soldier. This turn of events would end up redefining him as an all-American hero, or mark the end of his career as a rebel figure, depending on your viewpoint. For when he returned from two years as a GI, his destination was Hollywood where he would remain before donning leathers and making a comeback in the late 1960s as a born-again leather-clad rocker.

As for RCA, they would look in vain for another figure to generate the kudos and record sales they'd enjoyed in Elvis's heyday. (Perhaps the closest they came was David Bowie in the 1970s.) They remained his record label till the end, and continue to churn out reissues, remixes, and compilations today.

ELVIS' GOLDEN RECORDS

RELEASED: May 21, 1958
RECORDED: July 1954–September 1957
LENGTH: 47:03
LABEL: RCA Victor
PRODUCER: Steve Sholes

Side One
1. Hound Dog *Jerry Leiber and Mike Stoller*
2. Loving You *Jerry Leiber and Mike Stoller*
3. All Shook Up *Otis Blackwell and Elvis Presley*
4. Heartbreak Hotel *Mae Axton, Tommy Durden, Elvis Presley*
5. Jailhouse Rock *Jerry Leiber and Mike Stoller*
6. Love Me *Jerry Leiber and Mike Stoller*
7. Too Much *Lee Rosenberg and Bernard Weinman*

Side Two
1. Don't Be Cruel *Otis Blackwell and Elvis Presley*
2. That's When Your Heartaches Begin *Fred Fisher, Billy Hill, William Raskin*
3. (Let Me Be Your) Teddy Bear *Kal Mann and Bernie Lowe*
4. Love Me Tender *Vera Matson and Elvis Presley*
5. Treat Me Nice *Jerry Leiber and Mike Stoller*
6. Anyway You Want Me (That's How I Will Be) *Cliff Owens and Aaron Schroeder*
7. I Want You, I Need You, I Love You *Lou Kosloff and George Mysels*

Chapter 8

Elvis on Television

"They put me on television. And the whole thing broke loose. It was wild, I tell ya for sure. "
~ **Elvis Presley**

LEFT: Elvis and the band rehearse for *The Ed Sullivan Show*, October 28, 1956. *Bettmann/Corbis BE040199*

ELVIS ON TELEVISION

"Without preamble, the three-piece band cuts loose. In the spotlight, the lanky singer flails furious rhythms on his guitar, every now and then breaking a string. In a pivoting stance, his hips swing sensuously from side to side and his entire body takes on a frantic quiver, as if he had swallowed a jackhammer." ~ *Time* **magazine**

Elvis's hip-swiveling TV appearances not only inspired a generation of performers-to-be but affronted their parents. Eventually, cameramen were ordered to cut him off at the waist to avoid any unsavoury pelvic movements! But the man himself was unrepentant. "That's just the way I sing," he explained to TV host Milton Berle. "I can't sing any other way. I need my whole body."

Colonel Parker saw television as the ideal medium by which to promote his protégé and, once first RCA single ""Heartbreak Hotel" had been recorded in 1956, lined up as many shows as he could. First up were six separate appearances, two weeks apart, on the Dorsey Brothers Show, based in New York.

The Dorsey Brothers Show was well past its prime and ratings were perilously low, but it was the first time Elvis had been exposed to a national audience. He exploded onto the stage, attacking the songs with boundless energy and his sheer delight at being on television was evident. Surprising everyone in his entourage, he didn't sing "Heartbreak Hotel," preferring "Shake, Rattle, And Roll" which segued into "Flip, Flop, And Fly." The sparse audience had never seen anything like it before and responded with both applause and embarrassed laughter.

On the back of the television exposure "Heartbreak Hotel" went up the charts. RCA released the first album, a

LEFT: Elvis rehearses for his performance on *The Milton Berle Show* of June 4, 1956 with the Jordanaires and his backing group. *Michael Ochs Archives/Getty Images 74696932*

ABOVE: Elvis drops to his knees while on stage at his September 1, 1957, Seattle concert. *Seattle Post-Intelligencer Collection; Museum of History and Industry/Corbis MH001246*

mixture of newly recorded songs and unreleased Sun tracks. By the end of the shows, "Heartbreak Hotel" was Number 1 in the national singles charts and the album Number 1 in its chart. Hal Wallis, a Hollywood producer, had approached the Colonel, offering a screen test, and the trade papers were calling Elvis "RCA's new singing sensation."

The Colonel lined up a string of television shows including regular appearances on the Milton Berle Show and the Steve Allen Show, although the most prestigious, the Ed Sullivan Show, resisted.

Critical opinion was divided. Some thought him the most exciting performer ever to emerge from the American music scene and others thought him a joke. The latter criticized both his singing and his performance, calling it lewd. The press coined the epithet "Elvis the Pelvis" and used it ad nauseam. Elvis found it insulting. But controversy never harmed an artist's career prospects and

the thousands of column inches devoted to the pros and cons of the Elvis phenomenon simply fueled what was fast becoming a national debate. Juvenile delinquency was considered a nationwide problem and Elvis was seen as a contributory factor in its growth, especially as most of the teenage tearaways were now sporting Elvis Presley hairstyles and sideburns.

The next television appearance was the Milton Berle Show, staged on the deck of the aircraft carrier USS *Hancock*, berthed in San Diego harbor. The show was memorable because Elvis delivered one of the great Rock 'n' Roll performances of all time. Bill Black, caught up in the moment, rode his double-bass like a horse, slapping both sides of it, and the audience, made up of sailors and their girlfriends, went wild.

The performance is crowned by an unforeseen moment of high comedy when the wake of a passing ship rocks the *Hancock*, throwing all the TV cameras out of kilter and cut

ABOVE: In January 6, 1957, Elvis rocked 'n' rolled as usual in his final appearance on Ed Sullivan's TV show, but home viewers saw him only from the waist-up.
Bettmann/Corbis U1332940AINP

the head off Elvis and the band. After the show, the Colonel threatened Bill Black with the sack for the bass-slapping incident because it took the attention away from Elvis. Bill, chastened, never did it again. At least when the Colonel was around.

"Heartbreak Hotel" stayed at Number 1 for eight weeks, selling two million copies and earning Elvis his first gold disc. Life had become a frenetic round of gigs, television appearances and studio work, and the search was on for a follow-up single. They found it on April 14 at RCA Studios in Nashville, a ballad called, "I Want You, I Need You, I Love You." There were 300,000 advance orders, the largest in RCA's history.

The next Milton Berle Show proved to be a quantum leap in the Presley legend. Elvis sang a yet-to-be-recorded song called "Hound Dog," a Jerry Leiber/Mike Stoller blues shouter that had been a minor hit for Big Mama Thornton. For the first time Elvis ditched the guitar and, with freshly dyed black hair, delivered a performance that eclipsed everything that had gone before. His movements were less frantic and more calculated, now tailored to highlight the dynamics of the song. He punctuated DJ's machine-gun rolls with a blur of leg snaps that drew delighted applause from the audience.

Halfway through the song the band half-timed the tempo and Elvis went up a gear. The mood changed. He appeared out of control, totally immersed in the rhythm and the leg snaps, now slower, became overtly sexual. The audience was now in a frenzy, just where Elvis wanted them. He lowered his head, trying unsuccessfully to hide a smile. This was pure, unfettered genius.

Elvis frightened the life out of both the TV networks and the critics. The next day's press branded him "vulgar" and "obscene" and called for him to be banned. The Daughters of the American Revolution, a right-wing pressure group, released a statement saying they feared the effect he may be having on the nation's young people, and radio stations throughout the country dropped him from their playlists. The TV networks were caught on the horns of a dilemma. They had to show him because their ratings soared every time they did, but they were terrified of showing anything that would upset middle America.

They offered a compromise. They would continue to feature him on their programs but they would only show him from the waist up. Elvis was hurt and bemused, but the Colonel, who believed that any publicity was good publicity, was ecstatic. RCA, for their part, couldn't press records fast enough to meet the demand.

When his next single was released, a double A-side of "Don't Be Cruel" and "Hound Dog," the songs charted separately, "Don't Be Cruel" reaching Number 1 and "Hound Dog" reaching Number 2. Not even the mighty Ed Sullivan could ignore this and Elvis was booked for America's most important TV show. Shot from just the waist up, Elvis did a mesmerizing "Don't Be Cruel," watched by an audience that was estimated at fifty-four million, a third of the population of the United States and over eighty percent of TV viewers.

A January 1957 appearance on the Ed Sullivan Show would also prove to be his last for some time. The U.S. Army-bound Presley was now feted by his host, who had been recovering from a car crash on his debut show, which was presented by actor Charles Laughton. A now-recovered Sullivan told Elvis that "we've never had a pleasanter experience on our show than we've had with you," and the audience that he was "a real decent, fine

boy." Nevertheless, the uptempo numbers were still screened only from the waist up. Elvis might be off to serve his country in Europe, but his ability to inflame passions at home was still feared by that TV powers-that-be.

There is little doubt that the fast-growing phenomenon of television played a major part in launching Elvis Presley to superstardom. And while Colonel Parker would turn his attention to a bigger screen when Elvis returned from national service, certain television shows in the future would help re-establish the reputation of the King of Rock 'n' Roll—a man whose appeal to the camera was never in doubt.

BELOW: Some of the 23,000 fans in Maple Leaf Gardens, Toronto, Canada on April 3, 1957. Elvis's appearance in a shimmering gold suit caused so much squealing that few could hear him sing. *Bettmann/Corbis U1345259INP*

Chapter 9

Graceland

"I have enough memories of Graceland to keep my head spinning for the rest of my life. It was amazing. Filled with energy and excitement. Always something going on. Non-stop action and surprises." ~ **Lisa Marie Presley**

LEFT: The family—father, mother, grandmother, and Elvis—moved into Graceland in 1957. *Alison Wright/Corbis 42-15957128*

GRACELAND

"How many people have a family grave in the backyard? I'm sure I'll end up there, or I'll shrink my head and put it in a glass box in the living room. I'll get more tourists to Graceland that way."

~ Lisa Marie Presley

Visited by more than 600,000 fans a year for nearly three decades, Graceland is the Mecca of modern music. The sprawling fourteen-acre estate in Memphis, Tennessee, is a certified American historical landmark. It is situated on a road once known simply as Highway 51, now named in honor of the man who made it famous, Elvis Presley Boulevard.

It was here that Elvis would reign for two decades and even recorded his final two studio albums *From Elvis Presley Boulevard, Memphis, Tennessee* and *Moody Blue*. It would also be the scene of his death in 1977.

The grounds have a history that predate even the King. They were originally owned by one S.C. Toof who ran a cattle farm on the site in 1861. Toof was also the owner of a Memphis printing company of the same name and dubbed the estate Graceland after his daughter.

Grace's niece, Memphis socialite Ruth Moore, and her surgeon husband Thomas built the grand structure that millions now know as Graceland. The Moores commissioned local architects Max Furbringer and Merrill Ehrman to build the southern colonial-style mansion in 1939 and Ruth retained the name in honor of her aunt.

Ruth and Thomas had a daughter, also named Ruth, before divorcing in 1952. Ruth Jr. and husband Charles Cobb lived at the mansion for a time as newlyweds before Ruth Sr. decided the upkeep was too much and put the mansion on the market.

There was no shortage of potential buyers including U.S. department-store chain Sears and a party intent on opening a restaurant on the site. But Ruth Sr. had allowed a local church to operate on her property and it wanted to

LEFT: During 1956 it became obvious that the Presley household was too small. Here Vernon and Gladys display a stack of gifts representing a single day's worth from all over the U.S. addressed to Elvis. *Bettmann/Corbis U1324132*

purchase five acres of land, which neither Sears nor the restaurant were keen on. A third party wanted Graceland and was more than happy to share with the church. Enter Elvis Presley.

"She was the most wonderful mother anyone could ever have. She was always so kind and good." ~ Elvis Presley *Memphis Press-Scimitar*, August 15, 1958

After his breakthrough on RCA in 1956 it was becoming clear his modest three-bedroom house on Audubon Drive in East Memphis would no longer be a suitable abode. Fans gathered outside in their thousands and the neighbors naturally grew tired of the circus. Presley instructed his parents to look for a new property out of town.

The area was some twelve miles from downtown Memphis and was in theory a place Elvis could escape the throngs of fans that camped outside his current home. In the intervening years houses, apartments and shops have filled the distance between city and house to create an area far removed from the secluded location Presley chose.

Elvis bought Graceland for a reported $100,000 at the age of just twenty-two in March 1957. Ever the grounded family man, he moved in shortly after with his mother, father, and grandmother. The house would become symbolic of his meteoric rise and was a far cry from the two-bedroom shack in Tupelo, Mississippi, that he grew up in.

The iconic limestone structure would eventually consist of a mammoth twenty-three rooms including eight bedrooms and four bathrooms—and throughout his two decades in residence Elvis would set about decorating it in his own unique style.

Described by one detractor as "tacky, garish, and

ABOVE: Vernon Presley lines up a shot on the pool table which his son bought for the Presley Memphis home. *Bettmann/Corbis BE084179*

tasteless," the décor offers a window into the lifestyle of an icon. No two rooms are the same. The psychedelic wallpapering of the poolroom would be enough to put a seasoned professional off their game, and is in stark contrast to the grandeur of the black marble flooring in the decadent dining room.

The rouge walls and white faux-fur bed in Elvis's bedroom could not be more different from the avocado carpet and built-in waterfall in the den known as the Jungle Room and the gold and cream indulgence of the living room. However questionable his taste, Graceland was Elvis's safe haven, his escape from the intense world of fame.

The personality Elvis stamped on Graceland was apparent everywhere, including the entrance; wrought-iron

Elvis and his father are numbed over the death of Gladys. She died of heart failure following hepatitis. Elvis returned from Fort Hood on an emergency furlough to visit her but she died two days later. *Bettmann/Corbis BE032138*

gates were installed at the entrance to the property the year he arrived. The gates detail two figures playing guitars either side among a host of carefully crafted musical notes. They remain an iconic feature to this day.

Tragedy struck just a year after the family moved in. Elvis's mother Gladys died on August 14, 1958, after a summer-long battle with illness. In testament to the event's instant impact on his life, Elvis wanted to hold her funeral at Graceland but security fears dictated it was held at the local funeral home. It would be nineteen years before she would finally rest at Graceland.

The mansion would never be empty; many employees and extended family came and went. It wasn't long before Vernon Presley remarried in 1960, to Dee Stanley, and the newlyweds would move to a house just behind Graceland in 1962. This was a wedding present from Elvis, giving the lie to rumors he could not adapt to a woman replacing his beloved mother in his father's life.

Presley's young girlfriend Priscilla Beaulieu moved to America in 1962 to finish school under the condition she stayed with Vernon and Dee, but that prerequisite was broken and Priscilla was soon living at Graceland with Elvis. She would remain there for a decade until their divorce, during which time she would wed Elvis and bear his only daughter, Lisa Marie, in 1968.

Elvis would build a number of additions to the mansion throughout the 1960s, including the den at the rear known as the Jungle Room and a four-car garage at the north of the property.

In 1964 Elvis built the Meditation Garden as a place of reflection, and despite its twelve-foot fountain it would become the most poignant area of Graceland. The garden is now the final resting place of the Presley family; Elvis and Gladys were moved there from the nearby Forest Hill cemetery shortly after Elvis's death in October 1977, to be joined by Vernon in 1979 and grandmother Minnie Mae the following year. Perhaps most heartbreaking of all is a small, unassuming marker for Elvis's twin Jesse Garon, who never made the journey through life with the rest of the family.

The 1970s would see Elvis make more changes and extensions to Graceland, unaware of the limited time he

ABOVE: Elvis Presley with Priscilla and their four-day old daughter Lisa Marie. *Bettmann/Corbis BE020435*

would have to enjoy them as the issues leading to his untimely death began to take control. He would renovate his basement, including a poolroom and a TV room where, in typical rock-star style, he had not one but three televisions. The extravagance continued in 1975 as he built a two-story racquetball court complete with a Jacuzzi spa.

Two years later Elvis was found dead at the home he had so loved for two decades. While reports will always conflict, it is believed he retired to bed at around 7 a.m. on August 16, 1977, after enjoying drinks with his cousin Billy Smith and their respective partners. He was found five hours later and rushed to hospital where he was pronounced dead from heart failure.

ABOVE AND BELOW: Two views of the White Room, Elvis's living room in Graceland. At right the custom-made fifteen-foot sofa and coffee table. *Raymond Gehman/Corbis and Patrick*

Frilet/Hemis/Corbis AY008820 and 42-19834491

ABOVE: The TV room with mirror ceiling and walls. *Topfoto.*

His will entrusted his father Vernon as executor. Vernon had long handled his son's personal affairs and this would continue as he would be in charge of providing funds to the other beneficiaries of Elvis's will, Minnie Mae and Lisa Marie. Vernon, who passed away two years later, had already appointed Priscilla, among others, to succeed him.

The annual $500,000 cost to maintain Graceland would prove too much for Priscilla, who deemed it prudent to open the home to the public to safeguard Lisa Marie's future inheritance. It was agreed the mansion's first floor would never be seen by the public, and it is reported to have remained untouched since Elvis's death.

Graceland opened to the public in 1982 and quickly became a profitable venture, overseen by the business entity known as Elvis Presley Enterprises (EPE) that would manage the estate and its growing attractions.

EPE, led by Lisa Marie until 2005, has turned Presley's home into a multi-million dollar tourist attraction in its own right, receiving more than half a million visitors a year, with the White House the only home in the United States receiving more sightseers. The amenities include a shopping plaza and a hotel, while visitors can even view Elvis's personal jet planes *Lisa Marie* and *Hound Dog II*.

Though Lisa Marie still retains a fifteen-percent share in EPE and a hundred-percent ownership of the mansion itself with all the personal effects within, the grounds continue to drive the entire tourist industry in Memphis. It is perhaps a fitting final gift from the man who put the state on the map and delivered joy to so many through his music.

BELOW: Elvis's den received its jungle look in the mid-1970s. *Topfoto 1009613*

IN MEMORIAM

ABOVE: Elvis's jumpsuits are displayed during his seventy-fifth birthday celebration at Graceland, January 8, 2010. *Nikki Boertman/Reuters/Corbis 42-24127191*

ABOVE LEFT: Fans line up to enter Elvis's private plane named *Lisa Marie* near Graceland. *Lucas Jackson/Reuters/Corbis 42-18794374*

LEFT: Elvis died in 1977 and was buried with his family at Graceland. Today, he is one of the top earning dead celebrities, bringing in $55 million in 2009. *Nikki Boertman/Reuters/Corbis 42-24126603*

RIGHT: The graves of Elvis (second left), his grandmother Minnie Mae (left), father Vernon (second right), and mother Gladys (right) are surrounded with memorial tributes from fans. *Tannen Maury/epa/Corbis 42-18786615*

Chapter 10

The Army

"The army teaches boys to think like men." ~ **Elvis Presley**

LEFT: Pfc. Elvis Presley escorts his parents to town for a sneak preview of *King Creole*, June 2, 1958, on his first furlough. *Bettmann/Corbis BE032295*

THE ARMY

"(The Army) is an excellent experience. It lets you find out how other people think and live." ~ **Elvis Presley**

Initially, Colonel Parker wasn't too pleased with Elvis's military call-up. After all, the U.S. Army was taking his golden goose out of circulation for two, long years: more than long enough, in the here-today, gone-tomorrow world of Rock 'n' Roll, for Elvis to fade from public view. The Colonel had offered to pull a few strings to get him an exemption, but Elvis was adamant—he wanted to serve his country. And what's more, he didn't want any special treatment. He wanted to serve as a regular GI. That meant that, while he was in the army, there would be a complete cessation of his musical activity—no recording, no filming, no live performances.

The Colonel reluctantly agreed, but it didn't take him long to see the publicity bonanza that would accrue while Elvis was doing his patriotic duty. He also saw it as a way to steer Elvis away from the rebellious image. This could be the first step toward turning him into wholesome, family entertainer. This enforced, two-year hiatus could be a blessing in disguise.

The U.S. Army rubbed their hands with glee. They saw Elvis's recruitment as a golden opportunity to promote the service. They saw him playing an ambassadorial role, entertaining the troops, taking part in promotional

LEFT: Elvis leaves Kennedy Veteran's Hospital on January 4, 1957, after undergoing a preinduction Army physical. With him is dancer Dorothy Harmony. *Bettmann/Corbis U1121760*

Elvis with (L–R) Colonel Tom Parker, Eddy Arnold, and Steve Sholes at the RCA Recording Studios for his last recording session before joining the Army, March 10, 1958. *Michael Ochs Archives/Getty Images 74144635*

ABOVE: Elvis is the center of attention at a going-away party given by cast and crew of *King Creole*, March 13, 1958. Dolores Hart, left, and Valerie Allen help with the sendoff. He went to Graceland after the party to spend time with his parents before his Army induction date of March 24. *Bettmann/Corbis BE037005*

activities and extolling the benefits of enlistment, until the Colonel informed them that there would be no concerts, no photo opportunities and no press conferences. There followed a series of acrimonious meetings between the Colonel and the top brass, after which the army—completely outmaneuvered by the Colonel's superior strategies, tactics and deployment—surrendered unconditionally.

RCA weren't too happy, either. Army or no army, they expected Elvis to fulfil his recording commitments, as per contract. The market was crying out for more Elvis product, and they had to strike while the iron was hot. They offered a worst-case scenario. Two years without regular record releases would kill off Elvis's career. The public were fickle; they would forget him and move on to the next pop sensation. Then they offered a perfect solution. At their expense, they could fly Elvis back to America to record during his furloughs. No, said the Colonel, they couldn't. Moreover, if RCA didn't stop giving him a hard time, he would, when Elvis finally did get out of the army, take his boy to another record label.

RCA had no choice but to put up with it. But having taken away with one hand, the Colonel gave with the other. He informed them that Elvis had recorded a stockpile of songs that included "I Got Stung," "A Fool Such As I" and "Big Hunk O'Love," plus B-sides, to be released during his enforced absence. RCA were pitifully grateful for the Colonel's largesse, but conscious of the fact that they were now in his debt.

On March 24, 1958, Elvis reported to the Memphis Recruitment Office and became Private Presley. In a blaze of publicity—which pleased the army as much as it pleased the Colonel—he was photographed as a military barber clipped off the most famous sideburns in the world and stripped the iconic pompadour down to stubble.

In retrospect, this could be seen as the moment that symbolized the end of the dangerous rebel and the beginning of the wholesome family entertainer (the Colonel would see to that). It could be also seen as the high water mark of Presley's career (it would be all downhill from here, not commercially but certainly artistically).

Finally, if you were clairvoyant, it could be seen as the death knell of Rock 'n' Roll.

After his basic training at Fort Hood, Elvis was posted to West Germany to join the 2nd Medium Tank Battalion, 3rd Armored Division, the self-styled "Mailed Fist of Europe." Before leaving America, he did one final press conference which was later released as an EP. It sold over a million copies.

Elvis, and his fellow inductees, were shipped to West Germany on the troop ship USS *Randall*. During the voyage, he became friendly with Charlie Hodge. They had much in common. They were both from the South and,

before the call of duty, both had been working musicians. Charlie had brought his guitar with him, which is more than Elvis had done, and they spent most of their time singing, playing guitar, and swapping songs.

This attracted a great deal of attention and the captain of the *Randall* invited them to put a show together for the thousands of bored, sea-sick recruits on the brink of mutiny, who were temporarily in his charge. ("Invited," in this case, was a military euphemism for "ordered.") They had no choice but to agree, but Elvis, sticking to his pre-army pledge, refused to go anywhere near a microphone, preferring to play piano in the background

Elvis kisses his mother on the eve of his induction. *Bettmann/Corbis BE031605*

LEFT: Elvis is sworn into the Army by Maj. Elbert P. Turner (back to camera) on March 24. The twenty-three-year old was "dreading the haircut I'll get tomorrow," but hoped to be treated "no different than the other boys in the army." Assigned army serial number 53 310 761, he started his army life at Fort Chaffee, Arkansas. *Bettmann/Corbis BE031606*

BELOW: Vernon looks like any other proud parent as he examines his son's medals. *Bettmann/Corbis BE032296*

and ignoring all requests for him to sing. If he did it just once…

On October 1, 1958, the USS *Randall* docked in Bremerhaven, where the troops were transferred to troop trains which ferried them to their final destination—the U.S. Army base in Friedburg, just north of Frankfurt, that most American of German cities. After less than three weeks living in barracks, he applied for, and was granted, a permit to live off-base (so much for wanting to be treated like a regular GI). He rented a three-story house in nearby Bad Nauheim and started shipping his entourage in from

ABOVE: Elvis did his tank and basic training at Fort Hood, before being assigned to the 2nd Medium Tank Battalion, 32nd Armor, 3rd Armored Division in Germany. He arrived in Germany on October 1, and was stationed in Ray Barracks, Friedberg. He needed an escort as he arrived with his kit bag. *Güttert/dpa/Corbis 42-16734317*

Memphis. The first to arrive were his newly widowed father, his grandmother and two of his hangers-on, Red West and Lamar Fike, who immediately went on the payroll.

"How much shall I give 'em?" asked his father, who was in charge of the finances. "Give them enough to have a good time," said Elvis. "200 Deutschmarks a week?"

Rather than give it to them in weekly payments, Vernon—who didn't see the point of Elvis's entourage, who, it seemed to him, got paid for doing absolutely nothing—paid it out as per-diems, just a few deutschmarks at a time. Red and Lamar, as recipients of patronage, couldn't complain to the boss about his father's meanness,

so they privately seethed with resentment. They saved up their per-diems and, when they had enough, found the nearest bar and drank themselves to a standstill.

The rest of the entourage arrived and soon became a familiar sight in and around Bad Nauheim, always traveling in packs, always polite in a slightly threatening way. The locals started calling them "The Memphis Mafia." The entourage rather liked it, so they became, by self-appointment, "The Memphis Mafia." Elvis watched this with some amusement, like an indulgent headmaster policing an unruly playground. He rarely left the house in Bad Nauheim unless duty called, so the Memphis Mafia offered distraction from the tedious passage of time (shaving-foam fights were the favorite pastime or, depending on their mood, firework fights).

Charlie Hodge became a frequent visitor to the house, often staying overnight and sometimes weeks at a time, well on his way to being indispensable. Vernon loved him because Charlie, who knew hundreds of jokes, kept him laughing. Charlie fitted right in. "Elvis always kept his own world with him," said Lamar Fike. "He always kept his own bubble."

The house became a part of West Germany that was forever Memphis, Tennessee. But, while they were in Germany, the dynamic between Elvis and the Memphis Mafia began to change. Back in Memphis, they'd been old-school buddies, shootin' the breeze. They had their disagreements, but if things got a little tense and you needed to cool down, you could always go home and see the family for a few days. You couldn't do that in Germany, thousands of miles and an ocean away from home. There was no longer a safety valve. They were prisoners in the hermetically sealed house, totally dependant, financially and psychologically, on Elvis.

And Elvis was changing. He was becoming more demanding. He didn't issue direct orders, but might suggest during a conversation that something needed to be done and that it would be really nice if someone did it. It was just day-to-day stuff, rarely more than running errands, but it happened with increasing frequency and the Memphis Mafia started to feel put upon. If Elvis wanted them to

Bill Haley was in the middle of a European tour in October 1958 and Elvis went to his shows in Frankfurt on October 23 and Stuttgart on the 29th. *Bettmann/Corbis BE031886*

ABOVE AND RIGHT: Elvis trained hard and was a good soldier—as here training on a bazooka. It was after such an exercise—Operation "Winter Shield" in Grafenwöhr—on February 11, 1960, that he was given his full sergeant's stripes. *Corbis NA012536 and NA004542*

work for him, he should put them on a weekly wage instead of doling out occasional pocket money.

There was a simple explanation for Elvis's changing behavioral patterns. He was taking industrial quantities of amphetamine. Amphetamine galvanizes the central nervous system, speeds up metabolism and makes sleep impossible. It suppresses the appetite, causing rapid weight-loss, and prolonged use frazzles the brain. Unofficially provided by the Army, it was readily available to American troops on combat readiness, because it was the perfect battlefield stimulant. Soldiers under its influence didn't need sleep, didn't need food and didn't get tired. If they did, they just took another "purple heart."

So, whenever Elvis's regiment went on maneuvers, he was issued with his quota of pills. He liked amphetamine.

It gave him boundless energy and kept his weight down. In between manoeuvres, he continued taking it. Suddenly, the house was full of bottles of purple hearts, and Elvis was offering handfuls of pills to the Memphis Mafia and selected visitors. "Don't take too many," he'd advise, "or you'll be doing headstands in the hallway."

During his time in the Army, Elvis didn't once return to America, preferring to spend his furloughs hanging around the house, horsing around with the Memphis Mafia. And the Colonel never traveled to Germany, but rarely a day passed when he wasn't on the phone, planning and scheming, making sure Elvis had everything he needed and administering daily doses of long-distance intensive care.

From Elvis's point of view, the Colonel was the man who had steered him from obscurity to international fame.

Everything he had, he owed to the Colonel. He trusted him, even loved him, so the Colonel's word was law. He occasionally recounted a recurrent nightmare to which he was prone. During the nightmare, Elvis found himself in mortal terror, pursued, without rhyme or reason, by faceless assassins. Only the Colonel could help him. He had to find the Colonel. His life depended on it.

He spent the rest of the nightmare running in and out of derelict buildings, and through a labyrinth of endless corridors that always led to a dead end, while the faceless assassins got closer and closer (they were probably Pat Boone fans, he joked). But he never found the Colonel.

And he always woke up just before the faceless assassins nailed him. Make what you will of that.

One night, Elvis saw a TV documentary during which Jurgen Seydel, "the father of German karate," demonstrated the ancient martial art. Elvis was immediately hooked. As chance would have it, Seydel was a neighbor. He ran a karate school in Bad Homburg, fifteen miles away. Elvis drove over to see him and arranged some one-to-one tuition, twice a week. Karate became his passion, and he never missed a lesson. Seydel became a close friend and accompanied Elvis when he went on one of his occasional junkets to major European capitals.

As the day of his discharge drew closer, the Colonel started orchestrating the triumphant homecoming. He fixed up a welcome home TV special, hosted by Frank Sinatra. He primed RCA, making sure they had the studios booked, the pressing plants ready to roll, and he bombarded the press with exclusive stories that may, or may not, have been true.

Hal Wallis from Paramount arrived in Bad Nauheim, still emotionally battered and bruised after protracted negotiations with the Colonel which resulted in Paramount paying an absolute fortune for Elvis's exclusive movie contract (the Colonel had ratcheted up the negotiations by claiming that

ABOVE AND LEFT: Elvis at Ray Barracks. *Bohnacker/dpa/Corbis 42-16734316 and 42-16734331*

20th Century Fox were interested in picking up Elvis's movie contract, but it was all invented to unsettle Wallis).

Wallis, with a film crew in tow, was there to oversee the pre-production filming of German locations and army footage for Elvis' comeback movie *GI Blues*, a frothy, military rom-com. Elvis, meanwhile, was deciding what songs to use on his comeback album, when, suddenly, he was struck by a thunderbolt. And her name was Priscilla Beaulieu.

Chapter 11

Elvis and Priscilla

"Elvis brought out this mothering quality. I cut his meat up for him. I tasted it before he ever had it. I would fix his deviled eggs, cut off the top, put his butter in, prepare all his food as a mother would for a child." ~ Priscilla Presley

LEFT: Priscilla Beaulieu, daughter of a U. S. Air Force captain from Austin, Texas, lived in Wiesbaden. Elvis wears a 2d Armored Division patch in the photograph which must have been taken at Fort Hood before he joined 3d Armored Division in Germany. *Topfoto 0195801*

ELVIS AND PRISCILLA

"I lived a really wonderful life with this man and even after our divorce, it was incredible. We had a closer bond, probably because the effort was off and there was just a purity. We realized that we liked each other, and that's very special." ~ **Priscilla Presley**

The first time Elvis Presley saw Priscilla Beaulieu his world turned upside-down. "Did you see her bone structure?" he said to Charlie Hodge. "She's like the woman I've been looking for all my life."

It was love at first sight. But there was a catch. She was only fourteen years old. She was the daughter of Captain Paul Beaulieu, a career airman recently posted to nearby Wiesbaden. She was self-assured and independent for her age because, as part of a military family, she was used to being regularly uprooted and relocated.

When the family arrived in Wiesbaden, she naturally took advantage of the facilities available and started calling in at the Eagle Club, a community center for Air Force families, on her way home from school. She became a familiar sight in the snack bar and, as a strikingly pretty girl—at her previous posting she had been voted the "Most Beautiful" and "Best Dressed" by her fellow classmates— she began to attract the attention of a good-looking wheeler-dealer in his mid-twenties who introduced himself as Curry Grant, the entertainment director of the Eagle Club. She knew him by sight because she'd often caught him staring at her. But that was no big deal; she was used to men ogling her.

After a little ice-breaking small talk, Grant asked her if she knew that Elvis Presley lived just down the road? Was she an Elvis fan? Of course, she was. Wasn't everybody? She'd been delighted when her father had been posted to Wiesbaden because, she'd told her friend, she was going to meet Elvis. Well, said Grant, he was a good friend of Elvis. Would she like to meet him? Alarm bells went off in Priscilla's head. This sounded like a line. Yes, she said cautiously.

Grant, sensing her caution, went on to explain how he'd met Elvis. Elvis's father, Vernon, and Lamar Fike, his minder for the evening, had been guests at a charity event he'd organised. He and Lamar hit it off, and he'd been invited to a social gathering at Elvis's house. He'd got on with everybody and was now a regular visitor. This seemed plausible, so she agreed, but first she'd have to ask her father's permission. Grant asked for his telephone number so he could arrange it. She reluctantly gave it. If she'd refused, she'd blow her chance to meet Elvis.

Grant spoke to Captain Beaulieu, who agreed, as long as Priscilla was well-chaperoned the entire time, which Grant promised she would be. He also imposed a curfew, which Grant promised to honor. The following Saturday, when he knew Elvis would be home, Grant picked her up and drove her to the house in Bad Nauheim. Elvis was lolling in an armchair listening to a record of Brenda Lee singing "Sweet Nuthins" when Grant ushered her in. Elvis's jaw dropped. This was the most beautiful woman he had ever seen. He stood up.

"Well," he said, "What do we have here?"

"Elvis," said Curry, "this is Priscilla Beaulieu, the girl I told you about."

Their first conversation was about school. Assuming her to be older than she was, he asked her if she was a junior or a senior in high school? She cringed because she was still too young to go to high school.

"I'm still in the ninth grade," she reluctantly admitted.

"The ninth grade?" said an amused Elvis. "Why, you're just a baby."

"Thanks," she said, mortified.

"Not even Elvis Presley had the right to say that to me," she later recalled.

Elvis, now head over heels in love, went into amorous overdrive. Sitting at the piano, he sang her a selection of his hits, interspersed with romantic ballads, directly aimed at her. She felt embarrassed at being the center of attraction in a room full of male adults, all watching for, and judging, her every response. She thought the Memphis Mafia were creepy because they each seemed to be competing for their master's attention. These were grown men acting like sycophantic parasites. And the huge poster of a semi-naked Brigitte Bardot on one of the walls didn't help the ambience.

Sensing her discomfort, Elvis suggested they have something to eat. He took her into the kitchen and introduced her to his grandmother, who, it seemed, permanently lived in the kitchen. She cooked them bacon sandwiches smothered in mustard, one of her grandson's favorite snacks. Priscilla picked at one, while Elvis wolfed down five. Then they talked. Or rather, Elvis talked, and she, somewhat tongue-tied, listened.

For about two hours he poured out his heart, telling her of his hopes and fears. He wondered whether, after two years in the army, his career would be over. Well, he said, he could always go back to driving a truck. He was candid, confessional and funny. She knew he was trying to impress her and was flattered. She thought he was sweet.

Then an apologetic Curry Grant walked into the kitchen and announced that, unfortunately, it was curfew time. He'd promised Captain Beaulieu that he'd have her home by 10 p.m. Elvis pleaded for a little more time, but Grant said it was out of his hands. He suggested that Elvis

RIGHT: Priscilla is escorted off the tarmac by a military policeman after she had broken through a cordon and run towards the aircraft on which Elvis was returning to the United States. *Topfoto 0719689*

might like to ring Captain Beaulieu and personally negotiate a curfew extension, adding, helpfully, that he had the Captain's telephone number should Elvis wish to do so. Elvis declined. He said a reluctant goodbye to Priscilla and told her he hoped he'd see her again. Maybe she'd like to come over to the house again? Maybe he'd call her?

She got into Curry Grant's car and Elvis waved them off. They didn't make the curfew. They spent four hours stuck on a fog-bound autobahn and didn't get back to Wiesbaden until 2 a.m. Curry Grant had some explaining to do.

Priscilla thought that was that. She was struck by the bizarre nature of circumstances in which she found herself. Here she was, a fourteen-year-old girl, sitting around the house hoping that Elvis Presley would call. It was like a fantasy article from Teenage Romances. Elvis Presley, the King of Rock 'n' Roll, the most eligible bachelor in the world, was not going to call little Priscilla Beaulieu, of that she was convinced.

But he did—or, rather, Curry Grant did—the following day. Elvis, said Grant, would like to see her again. Would she like to come to the house again? Yes, she said, but again she had to clear it with her father. This time the Captain wasn't so amenable. It didn't seem right that his fourteen-year-old daughter should be spending time in a house full of grown men in the notoriously hedonistic, entertainment business. Priscilla assured him that it was safe, pointing out that Elvis's grandmother was always present. The Captain reluctantly relented, and the following weekend Curry Grant once again chauffeured her to the house in Bad Nauheim.

And, once again, the date started with Elvis sitting at the piano, singing songs to her, but this time the Memphis Mafia kept their distance. They were still there, but they didn't gather around the piano to listen to the boss sing (Elvis had obviously had a word with them). Suddenly, Elvis stopped playing and dropped a bombshell.

"I want to be alone with you," he said, "Will you come upstairs to my room?"

She panicked, fearing the worst, but stayed calm and said nothing.

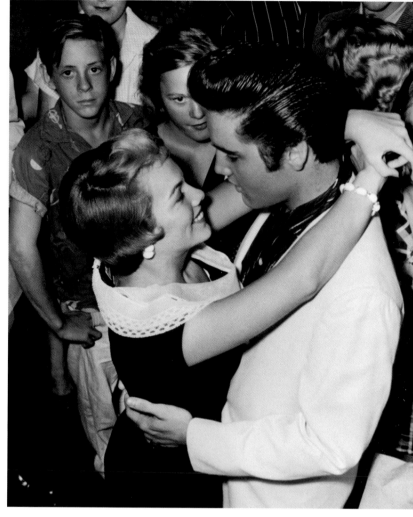

ABOVE: The girl he left behind ... Elvis and Anita Wood dance together in 1957. *Bettmann/Corbis BE031523*

"There's nothing to be frightened of, honey," he said, leaning forward and stroking her hair. "I swear I'll never to anything to harm you. I'll treat you like a sister." He sounded so sincere she agreed.

It wouldn't look good if they suddenly went upstairs together, he said, so why didn't she go up first and he'd follow shortly. He gave her directions and off she went, wondering whether the eyes of the Memphis Mafia were following her every step and imagining all the nudging and winking going on.

Once in Elvis's bedroom, she started nosing around. She discovered what records he played, what books he read and what clothes he had in his large wardrobe. She also found, and read, some love letters from Anita Wood, his current girlfriend who the press considered a serious contender to become Mrs. Elvis Presley on his return to American soil. The letters were just left on the bedside table, almost as if Elvis meant her to find them. And read them.

When Elvis finally walked in, he turned on the radio, which was tuned to American Forces Network, and they sat next to each other on the edge of the bed and talked. And talked. The time flew by and suddenly Curry Grant was knocking on the bedroom door, reminding them of the Captain's curfew. As she left, Elvis gave her a chaste kiss on the lips.

On her third visit to the house, she told Elvis that her father had imposed another condition. If these visits were to be ongoing, he'd said, then he thought it only right and proper that Elvis should personally pick her up and drop her off rather than delegating the task to one of his flunkeys.

"Okay," said Elvis. "Next time I'll pick you up."

When the next time rolled around, Elvis arrived outside the Beaulieu residence in his top-of-the-range white BMW. He brought Vernon with him for moral support. Priscilla answered the door and showed them into the captain's study. Elvis had left nothing to chance. He was in full dress-uniform and he'd brought a bunch of flowers for Priscilla's mother. The captain kept them waiting for the recommended time (as dictated by the implicit military protocols that governed social relations between commissioned officers and enlisted men), then he and Mrs Beaulieu walked in.

Elvis jumped out of his seat and introduced himself and "his Daddy." All the men shook hands. The conversation was stilted and mainly about matters military. Elvis told the captain about his latest assignment, on manoeuvres with the regiment scouts. Suddenly, the captain cut to the chase. Why would Elvis, who presumably could have his pick of all the starlets in Hollywood, be so interested in his daughter? Why Priscilla?

"Well, Sir," said Elvis, "I happen to be very fond of her."

Priscilla was an intelligent girl, he continued, who was very mature for her age, and he enjoyed her company. His fame meant he couldn't go out and socialize like other GIs serving a long way from home, so Priscilla's company helped ease his loneliness.

"I guess you might say I need someone to talk to," he said.

Elvis and Priscilla, who was a bag of nerves, waited for the captain's response.

Okay, he said, as long as Elvis himself picked up Priscilla and dropped her off. Elvis, pushing his luck, tried to negotiate a compromise. By the time he finished duty, he said, got cleaned up and drove over to Wiesbaden, most of the evening would be gone, so would it be acceptable for "his Daddy" to pick up Priscilla if he promised faithfully he would always drive her home himself? The captain agreed. As they said goodbye, Elvis offered one final reassurance.

"You don't have to worry about her, Captain," he said, "I'll take good care of her."

And he did. More than that, he put her on a pedestal. He considered her the most beautiful woman in the world, showered her with gold and precious stones, and indulged her every whim. Priscilla, a sharp cookie, took it all in her stride, which was just as well because she was stepping into a strange new world. A bizarre, hedonistic world in which anything and everything was instantly available at any time, night or day. It would take some getting used to.

The transport arrangements only lasted a few weeks. Priscilla became a daily visitor at the house and, when Elvis got fed up of the time-consuming drive back to Wiesbaden one night, he tossed the car keys to Lamar Fike. From then on, Lamar always drove her home. Vernon, never a man to pass up a chance to bunk off, started whinging about the tedious afternoon drive and soon Lamar was picking her up as well. It was breaking the captain's iron law, but that didn't seem to matter any more. By then, they were way beyond the captain's influence.

They spent most of their time in Elvis's bedroom, just enjoying being together. Sometimes it got a little frisky, but

promised each one that he'd recall them as soon as circumstances allowed. As the house emptied, Elvis got down to work. The Colonel, cranking up the homecoming publicity campaign, arranged a series of high-profile telephone interviews with American TV and radio stations, including Dick Clark on American Bandstand. Elvis did three or four a day, always, thanks to the different time zones, at weird hours.

The Colonel also arranged a farewell press conference, the day before Elvis flew back to America, at the enlisted men's club in Ray Barracks in nearby Friedburg, during which he answered the usual questions from an international press corps with his customary aplomb. But one set of questions caught him off guard.

"Who is Priscilla Beaulieu? Is it true that she's an officer's daughter? Is it true she's only sixteen years old? Is it serious?"

"She's a very nice girl," said Elvis. "Her family is nice and she's very mature for her age." It had been mutually arranged beforehand that, should the topic of Priscilla arise, everybody would stick to the agreed line—she was sixteen years old. If the press found out that he was dating an under-age girl, it could finish his career.

As soon as the press corps left the conference, the search for Priscilla's father began. They found him, and bombarded him with phone calls. How did he feel about his daughter dating the King of Rock 'n' Roll? The captain, now firmly onside and fully briefed, played it down. "There is nothing serious about this." he said. "The two of them have been great friends. They've had a real nice time knowing one another, but that's all there is to it."

After the press conference, Elvis drove Priscilla home to Wiesbaden for the last time. She was plagued by teenage doubts. Did he really love her, or was it just infatuation? Would she ever see him again? She had so many questions and Elvis, steadfastly non-committal, didn't offer any answers. Was he already distancing himself from her? He dropped her off, said goodbye to her and the entire Beaulieu family and drove off. After he'd gone, she wondered if it had all been a dream.

Elvis—conscious of her age and determined to play this one by the book—always backed off. There'd be plenty of time to make love, he told her. They had their whole future in front of them.

As the end of his army service drew closer, the Memphis Mafia, one by one, started to fly back home. He

Chapter 12

"Lights…Camera… Elvis!"

"I've had intellectuals tell me that I've got to progress as an actor, explore new horizons, take on new challenges, all that routines. I'd like to progress, but I'm smart enough to realize that you can't bite off more than you can chew in this racket. You can't go beyond your limitations. They want me to try an artistic picture. That's fine. Maybe I can pull it off some day. But not now. I've done eleven pictures and they've all made money. A certain type of audience likes me. I entertain them with what I'm doing. I'd be a fool to tamper with that kind of success." ~ **Elvis Presley**

"LIGHTS...CAMERA ...ELVIS!"

"He was an instinctive actor...He was quite bright...he was very intelligent...He was not a punk. He was very elegant, sedate, and refined, and sophisticated." ~ **Walter Matthau**

E lvis polarised America. You either loved him or you hated him. Whether you did so or not depended largely on your age. Teenagers adored him and grown-ups loathed him. The perfect rebel profile. The mainstream media, staffed entirely by adults, considered him a sociopath, a pervert, a malign influence on the impressionable young and a clear and present threat to the very fabric of American society, so—hovering somewhere between hostile and vitriolic—they never passed up a chance to ridicule him.

"Elvis the Pelvis" became the epithet that stuck. Elvis hated it. He thought it childish. But it sold papers, provided jokes for TV comedians and gave the Daughters of the American Revolution a focal point at which to direct their ranting and raving.

Meanwhile, the young began asserting themselves, and the schools became the inter-generational war-zones. Teachers, on the front line, faced daily skirmishes with rebellious pupils intent on disrupting and overturning the status quo. And all the teenage tearaways they faced wore a uniform. They sported heavily-greased, Elvis Presley hairstyles, wore their jackets and shirts with the collars turned up like he did and mimicked his menacing slouch,

LEFT: Elvis Presley promoting movie *Jailhouse Rock*.
Sunset Boulevard/Corbis 42-25492574

while curling their upper lip with contempt.

Elvis provided a template for the perfect juvenile delinquent, and juvenile delinquents, according to the adult world, were the enemy within. So Elvis became public enemy number one. And the end result? Everybody knew who "Elvis the Pelvis" was.

So it was inevitable that Hollywood would come sniffing around. The Colonel signed him to Hal Wallis at Paramount, who, rather than wait for a suitable vehicle to launch his movie career, put him straight to work on a black and white B-movie western called *The Reno Brothers*, starring Richard Egan and Debra Paget. Elvis was cast as Clint, the youngest of the outlaw Reno Brothers, who was destined to die violently in a last-reel shoot-out, giving Elvis his first crack at a death scene. Almost as an afterthought, four songs were crowbarred into the film and it was re-titled *Love Me Tender*.

To be fair to Paramount, the songs chimed perfectly with the mood and historical time frame of the film, and "Love Me Tender," which Elvis, as the ghost of Clint, sang over the closing credits, was a rewrite of the old Civil War ballad "Aura Lee."

Love Me Tender was released to mixed reviews but there were queues around the block at every movie theater it was shown. The film recouped its production costs in three days and the single release of the title song generated, for the first time in music-industry history, over a million advance orders. He got the gold disc before it hit the shops. The hostile press, who'd been willing him to fail, grudgingly admitted that the boy not only had some acting talent but possessed a promising, screen presence.

His second film was *Loving You*. With a plot loosely-based on Elvis's own rise to fame, he shared the bill with two Hollywood stalwarts, Wendell Corey and Lizabeth Scott, who made sure a cynical, wisecracking script came to life. It featured some great Rock 'n' Roll songs, including the iconic "Teddy Bear" and "Mean Woman Blues," which

BELOW: Fans outside the Paramount Theater, New York, promoting Elvis's motion picture debut, *Love Me Tender*. Bettmann/Corbis BE079215

LOVE ME TENDER

RELEASED: November 1956
RECORDED: August–September 1956
LENGTH: 9:31
LABEL: RCA Records
PRODUCER: Lionel Newman

Side One
1. Love Me Tender *Elvis Presley, Vera Matson*
2. Let Me *Elvis Presley, Vera Matson*

Side Two
1. Poor Boy *Elvis Presley, Vera Matson*
2. We're Gonna Move *Elvis Presley, Vera Matson*

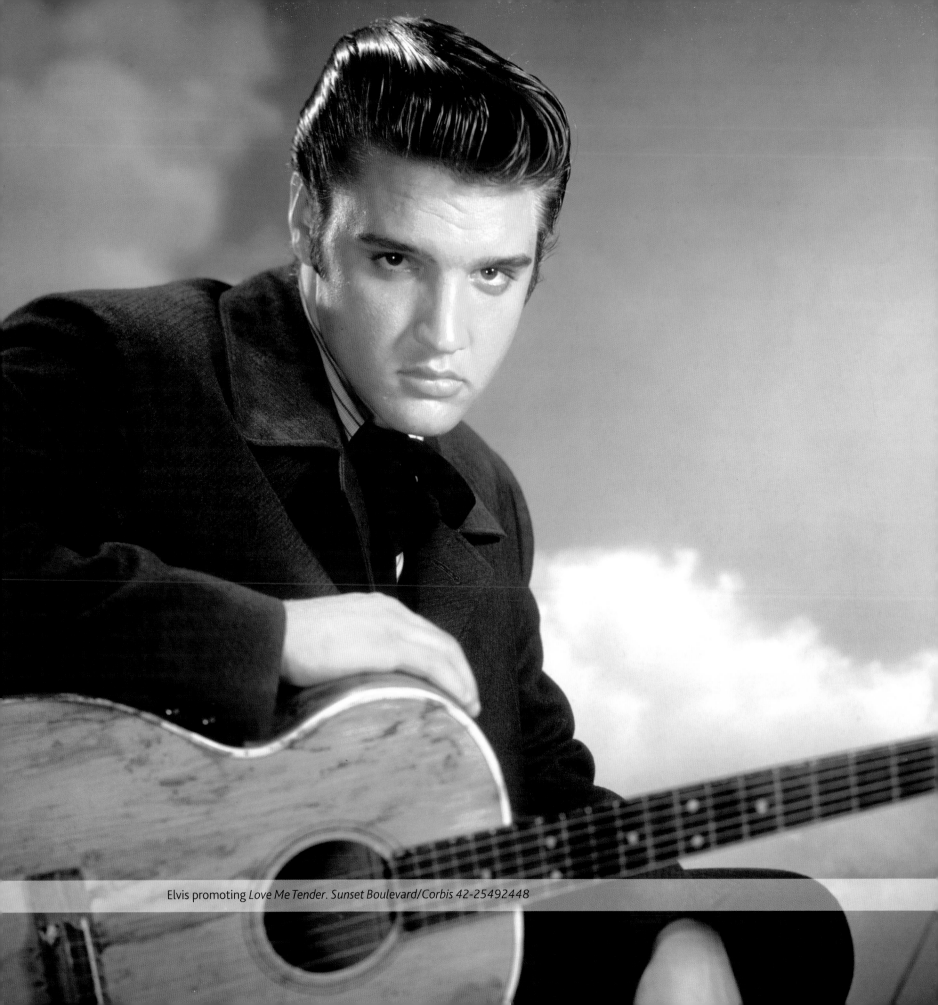

Elvis promoting *Love Me Tender*. Sunset Boulevard/Corbis 42-25492448

Elvis sang with mesmeric venom, giving those who would never see him perform live a glimpse of the sublime power he must have been capable of generating in his pomp.

"Teddy Bear" was released as a single and went straight to Number 1, selling two million copies and earning another gold disc.

The next film was *Jailhouse Rock*, and the title track alone was worth the price of admission. Jean Aberbach, the head of Hill and Range, Presley's publishing company, invited Jerry Leiber and Mike Stoller to submit four songs for the film. Leiber and Stoller—two white kids, not much older than Elvis—were the hottest songwriting team of the day. They'd already written several hits for Elvis, including "I Want You, I Need You, I Love You" and the biggest hit of them all, "Hound Dog" (which Elvis called "the Presley National Anthem").

Despite their productive association, Leiber and Stoller had never met Elvis. And they didn't want to. They thought he was a joke, a novelty act and, in their own words, an "idiot savant." When they'd first been invited to write a song for him, they were less than enthusiastic, so, as a conscious attempt to discourage him, they submitted an intentionally corny, hillbilly ballad called "Love Me." The strategy didn't work. Elvis either missed, or chose to ignore, the pastiche element and recorded it as a smoldering torch song. Another hit, another gold disc and a request for more songs. So Leiber and Stoller weren't surprised by the *Jailhouse Rock* commission.

Aberbach stressed the time factor. The songs had to be written and recorded before shooting began. He gave them a copy of the script and off they went. They ignored the deadline and pursued other projects. With only a few days to go before the start of filming, and still no sign of the songs, Aberbach snapped. He kidnapped them, locked them in a hotel room and forced them to deliver.

It was a close-run thing—so close, in fact, that there was no time to demo the songs. So it was arranged for them to go directly to the recording studio and personally sing the songs to Elvis. They weren't looking forward to it but they gritted their teeth and entered the lair of the "idiot savant."

ABOVE AND **BELOW**: Elvis Presley in *Loving You. John Springer Collection/Corbis JS434, Sunset Boulevard/Corbis 42-25493238*

ABOVE AND RIGHT: Elvis and Judy Tyler in *Jailhouse Rock*.
Bettmann/Corbis BE078899, John Springer Collection/Corbis JS1567126

Elvis introduced himself and, before starting, they talked about their favorite singers, particularly Ray Charles. Leiber and Stoller were surprised by Elvis's almost encyclopaedic knowledge of the blues.

"We thought we were the only two white kids who knew anything about the blues," said Stoller, "but Elvis knew all kinds of stuff. He knew our records, he was a workhorse in the studio and he didn't pull any diva numbers."

With Stoller on piano they jammed a little blues—then, the ice well and truly broken, they got down to business. They played him the new songs. The first was "Jailhouse Rock," which Leiber sang in his throaty rasp. As he sang it, Elvis started smiling. By the time they'd finished, he was grinning. "Okay," he said. "Let's make it."

While Elvis familiarized himself with the lyric, Leiber and Stoller ran the band through the song, worked on the

Elvis with Mike Stoller and Jerry Leiber on the set of *Jailhouse Rock*. Sunset Boulevard/Corbis 42-25493067

arrangement and stayed in the studio while it was recorded, cueing the band in on the changes. They were surprised by the leeway they were granted. Steve Sholes, the nominal producer, took a back seat and they assumed full control of the session. The song was soon in the can, to everybody's satisfaction. Then they rehearsed and recorded another two songs, again without interference from above.

As the session progressed, it became apparent that Leiber and Stoller had read the script. Elvis played an ex-con who becomes a professional singer, and the plot required different versions of some of the songs, each with a different level of competence, from amateurish to full-throated professionalism. On the early versions, they got Elvis to sing without artifice, even intentionally out of tune. This was crucial for plot development, but there was nobody from the film company present to oversee continuity so Leiber and Stoller stepped into the breach and found it an exhilarating experience. They left the studio looking forward to the next day, which turned out to be just as rewarding.

"The thing that really surprised us was that there was no clock," remembers Stoller. "It was amazing. Jerry and I weren't used to that."

Jailhouse Rock, the movie, was released to the customary tepid reviews. But it didn't matter, because the growing legions of Elvis fanatics all went to see it countless times and it became one of the year's most successful releases. "Jailhouse Rock," the single, rocketed to the top of the American charts, and, in the UK, it was the first single to enter the charts straight in at Number 1. It seemed that Elvis was unstoppable. Then came the bombshell. He was drafted into the U.S. Army.

It came at a most inconvenient time, although no time would have been convenient in the punishing Presley working schedule. But Elvis was due to start filming his next movie, *King Creole*. If he were drafted immediately the film would have to be canceled, putting hundreds of people out of work, so he was granted two months' deferment and the movie went ahead.

King Creole was based on the Harold Robbins bestseller *A Stone For Danny Fisher*, Elvis playing a nightclub singer caught up in the New Orleans underworld. The film was given extra gravitas by the presence of the peerless Walter Matthau as a ruthless mobster, and the divine Carolyn Jones (Morticia from TV's *The Addams Family*) as the femme fatale with a heart of gold.

Elvis acquitted himself well in a film that was a highly convincing drama, punctuated by great Rock 'n' Roll songs, like the title track, "Hard Headed Woman," "Crawfish," and "Trouble," a musical threat delivered with spine-tingling, testosteronic menace. "King Creole" was released as a single and, it almost goes without saying, racked up another gold disc.

The film was highly successful—helped, no doubt, by the blanket press coverage the drafting of Elvis had precipitated. It had transformed him from a dangerous juvenile delinquent with St. Vitus' dance into a great American hero, prepared to lay down his life for his country.

An intermission then ensued as Elvis boarded the troopship for Germany. His next effort, inevitably titled *GI Blues*, was some two years away—but his first quartet of big-screen productions could be looked back on with no little pride.

ABOVE : *King Creole* movie poster. *K.J. Historical/Corbis AAKZ001066*

Chapter 13

Elvis is Back

"Since the beginning, it was just the same. The only difference, the crowds are bigger now" ~ Elvis Presley

LEFT: After being discharged from the U.S. Army, Elvis grins as he hands his mustering out pay—$109.54—to his business manager Colonel Tom Parker, March 5, 1960, Fort Dix, NJ.
Bettmann/Corbis BE055328

ELVIS IS BACK

"I took the guitar, and I watched people, and I learned to play a little bit. But I would never sing in public. I was very shy about it." ~ Elvis Presley

On a cold winter's day, Sergeant Elvis Aaron Presley trudged through a carpet of thick snow into the paymaster's office at Fort Dix, New Jersey, to collect his demobilization allowance. The desk clerk gave him a cheque for $109.54, intended to give him enough money to get a bus back home. Acceptance of the money would be his last act in uniform. Plain, old Elvis Presley—no rank, no number—then walked out of the building to be greeted by a cheering army crowd, an unruly phalanx of press photographers, a military band and Colonel Tom Parker. Elvis waved the cheque in the air for the photographers.

"Don't forget my commission," said the Colonel, just loud enough for all to hear. Everybody laughed as Elvis, feigning resignation, handed the cheque over. Then the military band struck up "Auld Lang Syne" and Elvis and the Colonel walked, through a guard of honor with arms presented, to a waiting chauffeur-driven limousine. He stopped briefly to sign autographs for a gaggle of excited, teenage girls—daughters of the regiment who had slipped through the cordon holding back their parents. Then, with a final wave to the crowd, he climbed into the limousine and drove off the base, chased by a fifty-vehicle convoy of press and public. The King of Rock 'n' Roll was back on Civvy Street.

On March 20, 1960, Elvis started recording in Nashville. The sessions were arranged and conducted in

the utmost secrecy. The studio was booked under a false name, and even some of the session musicians were told they were being hired by Jim Reeves. Elvis had wanted his pre-army band, Scotty, Bill and DJ, but Bill declined because of prior commitments. His own band, the Bill Black Combo, was, by then, highly successful, racking up a string of hit singles. Bill's replacement was stand-up bass-player Bob Moore. Augmenting the trio would be pianist, Floyd Cramer, who'd played on "Heartbreak Hotel," country guitar legend Hank "Sugarfoot" Garland and the Jordanaires, who looked like a convention of undertakers but sang like Rock 'n' Roll angels.

As they set their gear up, they speculated about their mysterious employer. They all thought it was Elvis. It didn't take a genius to work it out. He'd just got out of the army, they assumed he was going the start recording again one day and most of the musicians had last worked together on Elvis's final recordings before he was inducted.

Then Elvis walked in, and it was as if the last two years hadn't happened. The crew was together again. They did some catching up. Elvis told them about his time in the army and his new love of karate. As chance would have it, Bob Moore, the new bass-player, was also a karate devotee. Once Elvis discovered this, he and Moore put on a demonstration for the boys that lasted forty-five minutes, fighting in the middle of the studio. Then they got down to work. They easily slipped back into the old routine. First, they sent out for hamburgers and fries, and while they ate they listened to demos of prospective songs, choosing the best and suggesting possible arrangements.

In the control booth things were getting tense. And overcrowded. Among those present were Steve Sholes, the producer; the Colonel and his assistant, Tom Diskin; Chet Atkins, the head of A&R of RCA's Nashville division; Freddie Bienstock, representing Elvis's publishing company Hill and Range; a couple of senior execs from RCA, and Bill Potter, the studio engineer. This was the moment they'd all been looking forward to for two long years. At last, they would get their hands on new Elvis product.

They'd all worked with Elvis before and knew it took a while before he was ready to record. So, with gritted teeth, they sat through the forty-five-minute karate demonstration and dutifully ate their hamburger and fries. By the time Elvis started recording, they were almost crushed by the weight of expectation.

The first song was "Make Me Know It," written by Otis Blackwell. It took nineteen takes before Elvis was satisfied, by which time those in the control booth were almost suicidal, having convinced themselves that Elvis had lost it. But the selected take, with a perfectly judged, exuberant vocal, said otherwise.

BELOW : Nancy Sinatra and Elvis Presley on his last day in military service, March 1960. Nancy had been linked to Elvis by the press and in 1968 they'd co-star in *Speedway*. *Corbis NA004536*

The next song, "Soldier Boy"—an unconvincing ballad that offered long-distance advice to homesick soldiers—didn't help matters. It took 15 takes before that was in the can. "Stuck On You," earmarked as a possible comeback single, followed. It is a laid-back, Rock 'n' Roll shuffle with a great vocal that hinted back to the pre-army glory days.

Then came "Fame And Fortune," intended as a B-side for the comeback single. It is a straightforward ballad but, for some reason, it caused problems and turned out to be another multi-taker.

The next song was "A Mess Of Blues," written by Doc

ABOVE: The Jordanaires. *Michael Ochs Archives/Getty Images 74278940*

RIGHT: Chet Atkins (center) with Steve Sholes (right) were both on hand for Elvis's first recordings after his spell in uniform. *Michael Ochs Archives/Getty Images 74251970*

Pomus and Mort Shuman, a new songwriting team signed to Hill and Range by Freddie Bienstock. As the band listened to the demo, a collective shiver went down their musical spines. This was something special. They couldn't wait to get their teeth into it. "A Mess Of Blues" is a low-down, dirty blues shuffle that was custom-built for Elvis, who delivers one of the great vocal performances of his life while the Jordanaires drive the rhythm forward with four-part harmony, lonesome train-whistle vocals. A couple of takes and it was in the can. This, surely, was the comeback single.

The last song was "It Feels So Right," a slow, blues with an hypnotic groove that crawled menacingly throughout the song. Elvis delivered an edge-of-the-abyss vocal that was little more than a demand for unconditional love from any woman within earshot (here "love," as it so often is, is a songwriting euphemism for "sex"). And that was it.

Bill Porter, sitting at the mixing desk, recalls the executive mood in the control room. "They didn't say anything, but they wouldn't sit down until Elvis got it down," he later said, "then they started talking about other things."

He did notice that Steve Sholes, who'd produced Elvis since he'd signed to RCA, deferred to Elvis on matters musical. Sholes was the first to admit he knew nothing about Rock 'n' Roll and had only assumed the mantle of producer because he had personally signed Elvis to the label and, having failed to find a suitable candidate in the rush to get Elvis into the studio, felt obliged to do it himself.

At the start of his very first session, which had produced "Heartbreak Hotel," Sholes had told Elvis to "do what you usually do." As a consequence, RCA made a fortune and this made Sholes one of the most successful record producers of all time. Sholes knew little about Rock 'n' Roll, whereas Elvis had, almost single-handedly, invented it, so Sholes, recognising this fact, surrendered total artistic control to Elvis, thereby ensuring that the magic moments kept on coming thick and fast, And that—whichever way you look at it—was a masterstroke.

When they left the studio the sun was coming up. Elvis had enjoyed the session, and was happy with the resulting songs. Steve Sholes took the tapes straight to RCA. This was the moment they'd been waiting for. The record presses were on hair-trigger response, the shipping department were looking forward some serious overtime, and the delivery trucks were parked outside the loading bay, with their doors open and their engines running. The RCA boardroom listened to the tapes and, in their infinite wisdom, decided that the comeback single should be "Stuck On You" b/w "Fame And Fortune."

The record sleeve made no mention of the song titles, because to print off a specific sleeve would have taken precious time and might have risked delaying the release, so the pre-printed sleeve humbly declared: "ELVIS' 1st NEW RECORDING FOR HIS 50,000,000 FANS ALL OVER THE WORLD." Within three days they'd pressed, packed and dispatched 1.4 million copies and "Stuck On You" earned him another gold disc.

Shortly afterward, Elvis and his entourage—which included management, musicians, and selected Memphis Mafiosi—booked into the Fontainebleau Hotel in Miami, Florida, a few days before the taping of the TV special. The Colonel had booked the entire top floor of the hotel, delegating a cluster of the Memphis Mafia to stand guard over the lift entrances, vetting the arrivals.

They'd traveled from Memphis by train to give Elvis a chance to spend some time with Scotty and DJ because

he'd sensed a little distance between himself and them at the recording session. Not only were they among his closest friends, they were crucial, particularly Scotty, to his music, wherever it led them. He'd never been in a studio without Scotty at his elbow, so he wanted them happy and on-side. It was time for a little bonding, and where better to do it than on a speeding train heading for their reunion gig? Scotty recalled the journey.

"It was just unreal," he said. "The only thing I can relate it to was reading about Lincoln's body going back to Springfield or seeing movies of Roosevelt's body coming out of Georgia after he died." Crowds had gathered at every level crossing and every station they passed through, cheering and waving placards on which were written declarations of love and good luck messages to the returning hero.

"Even through we knew the Colonel had gone ahead and let all those little places know that Elvis was coming through, still it was thrilling," said Scotty.

Their arrival at Miami's central railway station was scary. Thousands of hysterical female fans, all screaming at the top of their voices, fought to get a glimpse of Elvis, while a cordon of Miami's finest did their level best to keep them at bay. As soon as he stepped on to the platform, a

phalanx of burly policemen surrounded Elvis and, driving a wedge through the hysterical females, escorted him to a waiting limousine. Once Elvis had left the building, the hysterical females dusted themselves down and went home, allowing the entourage to process at a pace of their own choosing to their waiting limousines.

The first item on the agenda was a joint press conference to promote the upcoming TV special with Frank Sinatra, at the cavernous Grand Ballroom on the affluent Miami seafront. The participation of Frank Sinatra, who famously loathed Rock 'n' Roll, was not only a tacit acceptance of Elvis's musical stature, but implied equal status, something Sinatra only conceded to American

> ## "Rock 'n' Roll is the most brutal, ugly, degenerate, vicious form of expression – lewd, sly, in plain fact, dirty – a rancid-smelling aphrodisiac and the martial music of every side-burned delinquent on the face of the earth."
> ## ~ Frank Sinatra

presidents and Sicilian mobsters. Sinatra never missed a chance to publicly denounce Rock 'n' Roll, so Elvis expected a little friction. During the press conference, Sinatra was asked whether he still hated Rock 'n' Roll, given that he was now welcoming home its greatest exponent.

"I haven't changed my mind about the music," he said, managing to be both magnanimous and condescending at the same time, "but the kid's been away for two years and I get the feeling he really believes in what he's doing."

Also appearing in the show were Sinatra's Rat Pack, minus Dean Martin, who had prior commitments. The Rat Pack also hated Rock 'n' Roll—if Frank hated something, then the Rat Pack hated it too—but greeted Elvis like a long-lost brother.

The show itself—imaginatively entitled *Frank Sinatra's Welcome Home Party For Elvis Presley*—was standard showbiz television. Elvis, dressed in black tuxedo with matching pants, looked lean and fit. His hair—always a reliable barometer of his career prospects—was light brown, its natural color, and teased into a gravity-defying pompadour.

Sinatra introduced Elvis and the studio audience didn't need the held-up cue cards that exhorted them to "GO WILD." Suddenly, the two most popular singers of the twentieth century were standing on the same stage. And they were about to sing together. They did a two-song medley, during which Elvis sang Sinatra's "Witchcraft" and Sinatra sang Elvis's "Love Me Tender." The slowed-down, harmonized ending of "Love Me Tender" was particularly effective, eliciting sustained applause.

As the applause died down, Sinatra had an idea. "Man, that's pretty," he said. "Let's do that end again." So they did, and it brought the house down.

The Rat Pack played a prominent part in the show, but every time they appeared they engaged Elvis and Frank in long, tedious bouts of wise-guy banter. Elvis, good-humored and self-contained, more than held his own and even did a little dance with Sammy Davis Jr., who seemed genuinely pleased to see Elvis back in circulation.

Then came the moment everybody had been waiting for. Elvis sang two songs alone. "Fame And Fortune," followed by "Stuck On You." He sang the first with controlled passion and the second with a mischievous glint in his eye. Neither is a great song, but it didn't matter, because just seeing and hearing Elvis singing new material was more than enough.

The show was aired six weeks later, to great acclaim. But something was missing. The intensity had gone. Once, he had physically possessed a song. Once, his body movements and the rhythm of the song had seemed like a single entity. Once, he'd signaled a song's every nuance

ABOVE: Frank Sinatra and Elvis give a finger-snapping performance as they rehearse a song together. Trading hits, Sinatra performed a swinging "Love Me Tender" while Elvis did his version of the standard "Witchcraft." *Bettmann/Corbis BE024541*

LEFT: Mort Shuman sings and plays the piano at his home in Neuilly. Along with cowriter Doc Pomus, Shuman wrote over 500 songs in the 1950s and 1960s for such musicians as the Drifters and Elvis—including "A Mess Of Blues." *Pierre Vauthey/Sygma/Corbis 0000270784-006*

with an instinctive muscle twitch that was Rock 'n' Roll poetry in perpetual motion. But now, it looked like he was, literally, just going through the motions.

The spontaneity had been eliminated, along with the supple grace. It was replaced by a self-conscious, diluted version of the old Elvis that seemed to have been rehearsed, or, even worse, choreographed. The implicit message was clear: once I was dangerous, now I'm safe.

A week after taping the TV special, Elvis headed back to Nashville to record his comeback album, inevitably titled *Elvis Is Back*. Before he left, the Colonel took him to one side and laid down the contractual law. They owed RCA eight songs which, together with the four from the previous session, was enough for the album. So, no matter how many songs Elvis recorded, he should only give them the

BELOW : Nancy Sinatra leans close to her father at the rehearsal of "Welcome Home Elvis." *Bettmann/Corbis BE024553*

required eight. No more, no less. He didn't want to give RCA a free song.

Two songs were already inked in for the next session. "Fever" and "Are You Lonesome Tonight?" "Fever"—an R&B hit for Little Willie John in 1956—was chosen because, while stationed in Germany, Elvis had played the Peggy Lee version, which had been a mammoth hit, over and over until it threatened to drive everybody else mad. It was obvious he was going to record it.

Once informed of the fact, the Colonel ordered Freddie Bienstock at Hill and Range to contact the song's publisher and negotiate a favorable royalty deal, which he did. And "Are You Lonesome Tonight?"—a corny country song that had been a hit in 1927—because it was the Colonel's wife's favorite. It was the one and only time the Colonel asked Elvis to record a particular song. Elvis feigned shock, but agreed. The Colonel was delighted. He was gonna get lucky tonight!

The second session followed the same trajectory as the first. They started at 7.30 on a Sunday evening, Elvis and Bob Moore had another forty-five-minute karate workout, they sent out for hamburger and fries, which they ate while listening to demos. Then they got down to work. This time the first session line-up was augmented by another drummer, Buddy Harmon, and saxophonist Homer "Boots" Randolph, who went on to have a huge, solo hit with "Yackety Sax."

They started with "Fever." Elvis stuck to Peggy Lee's minimalist arrangement—lead vocal, double-bass, and percussion—which is so distinctive that it is nigh-on impossible to imagine an alternative arrangement. Bob Moore played the song's signature riff on stand-up bass, while DJ and Buddy Harmon combined to create a dramatic, percussive backdrop over which Elvis's sultry vocal was majestically relaxed.

The next song was "It's Now Or Never," an English adaptation—commissioned by Hill and Range—of "O Sole Mio," a Neapolitan love song much favored by operatic tenors. Elvis, seemingly influenced by Mario Lanza, sung it operatically, finishing the song in the obligatory manner with a high, sustained note that severely tested his lung capacity. It took him several attempts to get it. He got through the song easily but never quite nailed the high note.

Bill Porter, the engineer, suggested that, rather than sing the whole song every time, Elvis could just sing the high note and he could splice the two together. But Elvis declined the offer. "Bill," he said, "I'm going to do it all they way through, or I'm not going to do it at all."

Much to everyone's relief, he got it on the next take. This would be the next single. It was meant to be a watershed, and a watershed it was. It said goodbye to the Rock 'n' Roll tearaway and hello to the mature crooner. It ushered in a new ethos that abandoned Rock 'n' Roll in favor of dramatic power ballads. It was almost as if he were trying to prove to the many who doubted his ability to sing—a commonly-held misconception, fostered by a hostile press—that not only could he sing, he could sing like an opera star.

He recorded another six songs, giving RCA the required eight. Among the highlights were the Clyde McPhatter hit "Such A Night" and Lowell Fulson's "Reconsider, Baby." "Such A Night" is a breathless romp during which Elvis duplicates every nuance of McPhatter's distinctive phrasing and throwaway asides, while "Reconsider, Baby," an extended slow blues, features a blistering sax solo from Boots Randolph.

At four in the morning, Elvis, his contractual obligations now fulfilled, turned his attention to "Are You Lonesome Tonight." Once he and the Jordanaires had run through the vocal harmonies, Elvis asked for the studio lights to be dimmed and signaled a take. In semi-darkness, he counted the musicians in. Elvis didn't like the take and called for another, but halfway through the second take he stopped singing. The band stuttered to a halt. "Mr Sholes," he said, "throw that tune away. I can't do it justice."

Up in the control room, Steve Sholes was panicking. The first take had a few glitches but it was dynamite. Sholes wanted another take, so he asked Elvis to do it one more time because, he lied, the Jordanaires had made a few mistakes. Elvis reluctantly agreed and, still in semi-darkness, sang it once more.

ELVIS IS BACK!

RELEASED: April 8, 1960
RECORDED: March–April 1960
LENGTH: 31:54
LABEL: RCA Victor
PRODUCER: Steve Sholes and Chet Atkins

Side One
1. Make Me Know It *Otis Blackwell*
2. Fever *John Davenport and Eddie Cooley*
3. The Girl Of My Best Friend *Beverly Ross and Sam Bobrick*
4. I Will Be Home Again *Bennie Benjamin, Raymond Leveen, Lou Singer*
5. Dirty, Dirty Feeling *Jerry Leiber and Mike Stoller*
6. Thrill Of Your Love *Stan Kesler*

Side Two
1. Soldier Boy *David Jones and Theodore Williams Jr.*
2. Such A Night *Lincoln Chase*
3. It Feels So Right *Fred Wise and Ben Weisman*
4. Girl Next Door Went A'Walking *Bill Rice and Thomas Wayne*
5. Like A Baby *Jesse Stone*
6. Reconsider Baby *Lowell Fulson*

"That's a hit," Sholes said to Bill Porter. And it was. When it was released as the follow-up single to the highly successful "It's Now Or Never," "Are You Lonesome Tonight?" spent six weeks at Number 1 in the American charts. Nobody could sing a corny song more convincingly than Elvis.

As they left the studio, once again the dawn was breaking. It had been an extremely productive session. He'd finished his comeback album and had his next two singles in the can. It was time to head for Hollywood.

Chapter 14

The 1960s

"Money's meant to be spread around. The more happiness it helps to create, the more it's worth. It's worthless as an old cut-up paper if it just lays in a bank and grows there without ever having been used to help a body." ~ **Elvis Presley**

LEFT: Crowds were an increasing problem. *Bettmann/Corbis BE079073*

THE 1960s

"The next thing I knew, I was out of the service and making movies again. My first picture was called, *GI Blues*. I thought I was still in the army." ~ **Elvis Presley**

On April 21, 1960, Elvis arrived in Los Angeles to start pre-production work on *GI Blues*. He and his entourage had traveled by train from Memphis to Union Station in Los Angeles. The Colonel made sure the trip was well-publicized so that every Elvis fan in LA would be there to welcome his boy and ensure that, all along the route, there were crowds of placard-waving wellwishers at every level-crossing, hoping to catch a fleeting glimpse of Elvis.

Just before they got to Union Station, the LA Police Department diverted the train into a convenient siding. They explained that thousands of hysterical teenage girls had turned up to greet Elvis and they were having difficulties with crowd control, so it would be safer, for both the fans and Elvis, if they left the train and traveled the rest of the way by road. They'd hired a coach, they said, which was waiting at their disposal.

Elvis and the Colonel agreed. They didn't want to disappoint thousands of fans, but neither did they want press coverage showing injured teenagers being ferried by ambulance to the nearest hospital. So the coach took them to Beverly Hills, where they'd booked the top-floor of the Beverly Wilshire Hotel.

The pre-production period was not without its problems. Because of a union agreement, Elvis was forced to record the soundtrack at RCA Studios on Hollywood Boulevard, instead of his preferred Record Recorders in Nashville, where he felt most comfortable. He told Paramount he didn't think the songs he was scheduled to record were strong enough, and he was particularly disappointed there were no Leiber and Stoller songs and only one from Pomus and Shuman. He didn't like the script either. His character was bland and the plot flimsy. And if it was supposed to be a frothy comedy, then the script wasn't funny enough. But Paramount told him it was too late in the day to change anything. He tried to enlist the help of the Colonel, but the Colonel's hands were contractually tied (or so he said).

Elvis didn't like the unfamiliar RCA studio, but persevered. But the finished product, in Elvis's opinion, was inferior songs recorded in an unsuitable studio. So, behind Paramount's back and at his own expense, he booked Radio Recorders and, during breaks in shooting, returned to Nashville to re-record most of the soundtrack. Even if the songs were lousy, at least they'd be recorded properly.

One day, the hotel manager had a discreet word with Elvis. Fellow guests had complained about the constantly blaring music and raucous behavior, especially the impromptu water-pistol fights that broke out in the hotel lobby. Their fellow guests were also uncomfortable with the round-the-clock stream of Hollywood starlets arriving and departing. And he himself was concerned about the smashed furniture the maids regularly found in their rooms, the result of over-enthusiastic karate contests.

Elvis apologized, offered to pay for the damages and promised a change in behavior, but nothing changed. "We lived on amphetamines," said Joe Esposito, a trusted lieutenant. "None of us slept for more than a few hours at a time. At five o'clock each morning we'd report to the set, then spend the rest of our time screwing around."

As the film progressed Elvis became more and more disillusioned. The film was going to be a disaster, and there was nothing he could do about it. "I'm locked into this thing," he said.

On the last day of the shoot, Elvis's first instinct was to high-tail it back to Memphis, but Paramount asked him to stick around for an extra week just in case any scenes had to be re-shot. But Elvis needed a break, so he decided to drive to Las Vegas for the weekend, taking the full entourage with him. They left in convoy, looking forward to a high-rolling time, but returned to LA when Elvis's cousin Gene forgot to bring the amphetamines.

Meanwhile, "Stuck On You," which had topped the Billboard charts, had been totally eclipsed by the release of "It's Now Or Never," the flagship single of the "new"

ABOVE AND LEFT: Elvis in costume for *GI Blues*. Both: *Sunset Boulevard/Corbis 42-25697494 and 42-25697493*

Elvis Presley in *Flaming Star* the violent story of half-breed Pacer Burton. *Sunset Boulevard/Corbis 42-25697420*

Elvis. It sold five million copies in America and a million in Britain. Similar sales figures came in from all over the world, making it the second most successful song in recording history after Bing Crosby's "White Christmas." The "new" Elvis was outselling the "old."

His next film was *Flaming Star*, the violent story of Pacer Burton, a "half-breed" with a white father and a Kiowa mother living in the white community. When the Kiowas go on the warpath, Pacer, played by Elvis, has to decide which side he's on (the role was originally offered to Marlon Brando, but he'd turned it down, so Elvis stepped into the breach). It was written by two seasoned screenwriters, Clair Huffaker, who'd written the original novel, and Nunnally Johnson, who'd written the screenplay for the Oscar-winning *Grapes Of Wrath*, and directed by Don Siegel, who went on to direct Clint Eastwood's *Dirty Harry* films. So this was a serious movie, requiring serious acting and minimal singing.

Apart from the title track, there was only one song in the film, a barn-dance tune which Elvis sang at his mother's birthday party in the Burtons' log cabin. The reason for this change of approach was simply a change of studio. Paramount had sold Elvis to 20th Century Fox for a back-to-back, two-picture deal. Different company, different ethos.

The film was shot on the Conejo Movie Ranch, just outside LA so, once again, they booked the top-floor at the Beverly Wilshire Hotel. This time, the hotel management were zero-tolerant of their high jinks and looked for a reason to evict them. They didn't have to wait long. One day, Tuesday Weld, a Hollywood starlet Elvis was dating, arrived in the lobby, on her way to a rendezvous with Elvis. She was a regular visitor but this time, for some reason, hotel security refused to grant her entry. She threw the mother of all tantrums, causing sustained chaos and much embarrassment. As a result, Elvis was evicted. He found a big house in Bel Air, owned by the Shah of Iran, on a six-month lease, which was perfect. It was in its own grounds, some distance from their nearest neighbors, so now they could turn up the sound system and do some serious partying.

ABOVE: Promotional shot for *Flaming Star*. Sunset Boulevard/Corbis 42-25697402

Once they started shooting the film, the downside was revealed. Don Siegel, who'd tried to convince 20th Century Fox that Elvis would be a disaster in the role, treated him like a dumb, country hick just off the bus. So, just to irritate him, that's exactly what Elvis pretended to be. Siegel hated Rock 'n' Roll, and was on record as calling Elvis "a laughing stock."

But they were both professionals, so Elvis and Siegel had no choice but to establish a working relationship even if it was based on mutual loathing and orchestrated indifference. But there were consolations. Siegel didn't seem to realize when he was the subject of mockery and took everything Elvis said at face value, triggering much stifled amusement.

The film ended with Elvis, fatally wounded, riding off into the sunset to look for his *Flaming Star* of death, after delivering the film's final line, which managed to be both trite and patronizing.

"Maybe someday, somewhere," he croaked, "people will understand folks like us."

Flaming Star had its flaws, but it was a joy to see Elvis doing a role with some meat on its bones. And, looking on the bright side, it was a quantum leap from the anodyne *GI Blues*, which had yet to be released.

Back in the real world, "Are You Lonesome Tonight?" topped the *Billboard* charts for six weeks, and Elvis recorded his next album, "His Hand In Mine," a collection of religious songs intended as a Christmas release. It was recorded in a single, overnight session in Nashville. So long was the session that, before the end, Chet Atkins had to go home to bed and Steve Sholes went on strike. But Elvis seemed to thrive on these marathon sessions, often singing for twelve hours at a stretch without loss of vocal quality. The man must have had a cast-iron larynx.

A week later, he arrived in LA to start pre-production for *Wild In The Country*, his second film for 20th Century

Fox. The *GI Blues* soundtrack album had just been released ahead of the movie, and was soon outselling "Elvis Is Back," further confirmation that the Colonel's plan was working.

Wild In The Country, written by celebrated playwright Clifford Odets, was the story of a budding author torn between the love of three women, played by Tuesday Weld, Millie Perkins, and Simone Signoret, the oldest and most exotic of the trio. Securing Signoret's involvement was seen as something of a coup because of her formidable international reputation and the fact that the French actress rarely accepted Hollywood's offers of work.

It looked good on paper. But just a few days before shooting began, Signoret pulled out and Odets was sacked. Signoret was replaced by Hope Lange, who delivered a solid performance but lacked the innate sensuality that the role required. Odets left an unfinished script (probably the reason he was fired), but there wasn't time to hire another writer so they padded it out with additional Elvis songs.

Unsurprisingly, the film was a mess. It was disjointed, oddly subdued, over-ran the shooting schedule and went way over budget. Millie Perkins summed it up: "I think that everybody thought we were classier, so much better than all those other Elvis Presley movies," she said. "Everyone was going around patting themselves on the back for being artists." And Elvis? "He never used his star power on the set. Maybe he should have."

GI Blues was released and went to Number 2 in *Variety*'s weekly chart of top-grossing films, thanks no doubt to the Colonel's last-minute promotional drive, which involved giving out one hundred thousand paper army hats to the public. It was expensive, but the Colonel got RCA to pay for it after Hal Wallis had emphatically refused.

"Surrender" was selected as the follow-up to "Are You Lonesome Tonight?" The song, another anglicized version of a Neapolitan ballad, was a shameless attempt by Hill and Range to capitalize on the "It's Now Or Never" formula. But Hill and Range, by accident or design, pulled off a winner by commissioning Doc Pomus and Mort Shuman to do it, thereby ensuring that the final result was both credible and artistically sound. "Surrender" failed to match the astronomical sales of "It's Now Or Never," but it still spent weeks at Number 1 on the Billboard charts.

Having honored the 20th Century Fox two-picture deal, Elvis returned to Paramount for his next film, *Blue Hawaii*, which was loosely based on a 1937 film starring Bing Crosby called...*Blue Hawaii*. Hal Wallis had been nurturing a cinematic dream—the soundtrack of a Bing Crosby picture starring Elvis Presley. The Colonel loved the idea.

Wallis hired Joseph Lilley as music supervisor. Lilley had already worked on five Bing Crosby films, so who better to re-create a Bing Crosby soundtrack? He was a stickler for musical authenticity, so hired the very best Hawaiian session musicians. The soundtrack included several English-language/European-music hybrids, including "Can't Help Falling In Love," which remained a highlight of Elvis's live show for the rest of his life. The closest the soundtrack got to Rock 'n' Roll was "Rock-a-Hula Baby," which Elvis sang with his tongue firmly in cheek. They were all good songs but they were the wrong kind of songs.

Blue Hawaii is a run-of-the-mill Hollywood, musical comedy with lavish, production values. Light in character and devoid of emotion, Elvis sleepwalks his way through the exotic, Hawaiian locations, leaving no shadow. The film is vacuous, unthreatening, light entertainment. Just what Hal Wallis and the Colonel wanted.

On its release, *Blue Hawaii* was Elvis's biggest hit, heading *Variety*'s top-grossing chart. The soundtrack album went straight to Number 1 in the Billboard charts, outselling all of his studio albums. Hal Wallis and the Colonel were delighted. Now the path ahead was clear. The formula was established. What the public obviously wanted was Elvis singing meaningless songs in exotic locations.

The Colonel had achieved his goal. Elvis Presley had become an all-round family entertainer.

LEFT: Elvis with director Don Siegel on the set of *Flaming Star*. *Michael Ochs Archives/Sunset Boulevard/Corbis 42-25697421*
RIGHT: Elvis and Joan Blackman in a romantic beach scene from *Blue Hawaii. Bettmann/Corbis SF36265*

Chapter 15

In the Doldrums

"Then I made some movies, you know *GI Blues* and *Blue Hawaii* and several pictures that did very well for me. But as the years went by, I really missed the people, the audience contact. I was really gettin' bugged. I was doing so many movies and couldn't really do what I could do. They'd say, 'Action!' and I'd go, 'Whop, whop, ump'." ~ **Elvis Presley**

LEFT: Elvis 1966. *Bettmann/Corbis U1507670*

IN THE DOLDRUMS

"I sure lost my musical direction in Hollywood. My songs were the same conveyer belt mass production, just like most of my movies were. " ~ Elvis Presley

The commercial success of *Blue Hawaii* was both a blessing and a curse. A blessing for the Colonel and a curse for Elvis. For the Colonel—for whom the generation of new income streams was a primal instinct—it was purely economics. For Elvis—for whom the creation of trailblazing, epoch-defining music was the justification of his existence—it was, or should have been, purely artistic. The music is everything, Elvis might have argued, and without it I am nothing. To which the Colonel would have offered an incontrovertible fact: Hollywood paid better than Tin Pan Alley.

So the Colonel took Elvis, knocked off the edges, nullified the sexual menace and, avoiding any hint of artistic controversy, headed for Hollywood and the big bucks. The magic formula—established with *Blue Hawaii*—always contained the following elements: exotic locations (usually Hawaii); a bevy of wholesome, bikini-clad floozies (all in love with our hero); some sort of dangerous, manly pursuit (usually involving racing cars, motorboats, motorcycles, or helicopters); a toe-to-toe brawl with a love rival (Elvis always won, due to his superior karate skills); and a clutch of insipid, nondescript, anodyne songs (usually sung to an ultra-cute, Polynesian child, holding a cuddly toy).

The Colonel exerted total control over Elvis's recorded output. Acting on his orders, Hill and Range vetted the songs Elvis was offered, ensuring his recorded output wouldn't challenge even the most casual listener. Deprived of songs from the best writers—who refused to sign half

their copyrights away—his output declined in both quality and frequency. And when the records were released, Elvis was puzzled. Songs that had sounded great in the studio sounded unbalanced when he heard them on the radio. The drums were never loud enough, and the vocal seemed to swamp the backing track. He began to distrust his own ears. Then it dawned on him. These weren't his mixes. RCA were secretly remixing his records before their release.

Elvis phoned them up. They categorically denied the charge. Extensive enquiries finally revealed the culprit. It was the Colonel. Once Elvis had finished an album, the Colonel would take it back into the studio and remix it, jacking up the vocal and pushing the instrumentation further into the background. When confronted, he was unrepentant. His defence relied on a skewed piece of addled logic: Elvis was a successful singer because people liked his voice, so the louder it was the more they'd like it.

During the previous decade, the release of an Elvis Presley record had been an eagerly awaited cultural event, but now his records came and went seemingly unnoticed. Subject to the law of diminishing returns, his fan-base dwindled and he was written off by the new generation of music critics, for whom he was an irrelevance. The Beatles had conquered the world and changed the face of music, so why listen to Elvis when you could listen to the Beatles?

Live performance wasn't even considered because, for the Colonel, it was an uncontrolled environment with too many unpredictables. Apart from a charity gig he'd done in

Honolulu, as part of the Blue Hawaii promotional drive, Elvis hadn't done a live gig since the army. If he did possess a burning desire to play in front of his adoring public, he kept it well hidden.

The Colonel's strategy, although initially successful, was now in ruins. People stopped going to see Elvis's films, his record sales plummeted and he was increasingly regarded as an artist whose time had passed. The King of Rock 'n' Roll was in danger of becoming a has-been.

In May 1967, Elvis married Priscilla Beaulieu at a

BELOW: Elvis surrounded by actresses Jenny Maxwell, Pamela Austin, Joan Blackman, Darlene Tompkins, and Christian Kay on the set of *Blue Hawaii. Sunset Boulevard/Corbis 42-25697237*

ABOVE and RIGHT: Elvis at Paramount Studios for *Girls! Girls! Girls!*, April 1962. Both: *Michael Ochs Archives/Corbis 42-17853569 and 42-25697571*

private ceremony in Las Vegas, and the happy couple honeymooned in Palm Springs. They'd stayed in touch after he'd left her in Germany, by way of phone calls, letters and—having first agreed to abide by Captain Beaulieu's comprehensive list of stringent conditions—occasional visits to Graceland when Elvis tended to treat her like a trophy to be displayed. But, while he avoided any hint of commitment, he found himself edging towards it. His closest circle of friends were subject to endless "Should I? Shouldn't I?" conversations. To everyone's relief, he finally made up his mind and popped the question.

So private was the ceremony that not even the Memphis Mafia were invited. The Colonel was delegated to inform them, which he did, wisely, by telephone. Red West, the most volatile, erupted. Elvis had often promised him that if ever he got married, Red would be his best man—now he wasn't even invited to the ceremony. Red blamed the Colonel, while the rest of the boys, masking their disappointment, accepted the decision with feigned equanimity.

Elvis later admitted that Red should have been invited to the ceremony. But if he'd invited Red, he'd have had to invite all of them, and then the ceremony would no longer have been private. But, as he further admitted, he should have taken a stand. Which suggests that the Memphis Mafia's exclusion was the Colonel's idea. Or maybe it was Priscilla's. She'd always found the Memphis Mafia's constant presence intrusive, so maybe she didn't want them there at what must have been the most intimate moment in her life.

But the awful possibility must have crossed her mind that, by marrying Elvis, she was also marrying the Memphis Mafia.

By mid-1967, it became apparent to everybody, even the Colonel, that Elvis's career was in terminal decline. His films were playing to dwindling audiences, and the hits had dried up (RCA even offered to build him a studio in Graceland, hoping to stir his creative juices, but Elvis refused). He was contractually obligated to churn out the films, so Elvis and the Colonel turned their attention to recording.

ABOVE: Elvis on a police motorcycle in 1963's *It Happened At The World's Fair*. Sunset Boulevard/Corbis 42-25697591

RIGHT: Elvis and Ann-Margret in a scene from *Viva Las Vegas*, 1964. Bettmann/Corbis BE078182

They decided to change their approach for the next album. New studio (RCA Studios on Los Angeles, replacing Radio Recorders in Nashville), new musicians (LA session musicians, instead of Elvis's usual suspects), new producer (Felton Jarvis, a new hotshot who'd just produced "Sheila," a mammoth hit for Tommy Roe), and, for the first time, an arranger (Billy Strange, who'd been Nancy Sinatra's arranger on her worldwide hit "These Boots Are Made For Walking").

Elvis drew up a list of prospective songs, so that Freddie Bienstock at Hill and Range could negotiate advance publishing deals favorable to Elvis (if you don't give me half your copyright, then Elvis won't record your song. Most publishers agreed, because fifty percent of an Elvis hit record is better than a hundred percent of nothing). The list included "The Wonder Of You," "From A Jack To A King," and "Guitar Man," a recent, self-penned hit for singer/guitarist Jerry Reed, an RCA label-mate.

But on the morning of the day they were due to start recording, with some of the principals yet to arrive in LA, Richard Davis, an occasional member of the Memphis Mafia, while driving out of Elvis's rented Bel-Air house, knocked down and killed their Chinese gardener. The Colonel, fearful of an expensive lawsuit, cancelled the sessions and everybody headed back to Memphis.

A month later they were back in Radio Recorders in Nashville, where Elvis, accompanied by the usual suspects and minus Billy Strange, started to record his next album. "Guitar Man"—a great, alpha male rock song—was intended to be the centerpiece of the album. Elvis, who'd never met Reed, heard the song on the radio, and loved it. It was the first song on the agenda but they couldn't come up with a satisfactory arrangement. Hardly surprising, given that Reed's highly individual guitar-playing was a crucial part. Without it, the song just wasn't going to work.

So Elvis hired Jerry Reed. But he wasn't an easy man to pin down. Reed's management said that Jerry had gone off on one of his fishing trips. He was alone in the wilderness, and there was no telephone at the cabin he used as a base. They could send a messenger up to the cabin, they said, but they couldn't guarantee anything. Try, said Elvis.

Viva Las Vegas was called *Love in Las Vegas* in the UK. *Sunset Boulevard/Corbis* 42-25697738

The following day, the Alabama Wildman arrived at the studio. He'd driven straight from the cabin and was still wearing his fishing gear. He hadn't shaved for weeks, he was flecked with mud, and he smelt of fish.

"What is *that*?" said Elvis, when he first saw him. Then Reed strapped on a guitar and, immediately, everything clicked into place. The resulting record was, by common consensus, the best thing Elvis had recorded in years.

This was the moment when Freddie Bienstock, from Hill and Range, entered the fray. He was late. He should have been at the studio from the start, supervising the song selection. The first thing he heard was the playback of "Guitar Man." "Guitar Man"? He couldn't remember doing a publishing deal for "Guitar Man." To his horror, he realized that he'd forgotten to do so, and Elvis had recorded a song he hadn't authorized. Somewhat optimistically, he tried to do a retrospective deal with Reed, but Reed refused and threatened to walk out.

At long last, Elvis put his foot down. He loved the song, he told Bienstock, and, not only was it going to be on the album, it was going to be his next single. Bienstock, preferring discretion to valor, had no choice but to back down, resigning himself to the roasting he would surely receive from the Colonel.

Jerry Reed agreed to stay for the rest of the session and they continued recording. Then, as if to compound Bienstock's misery, they recorded another unauthorized song. This time plucked out of the air by Elvis, it was the Jimmy Reed blues standard "Big Boss Man." With Jerry Reed to the fore again, it was soon in the can. Bienstock was mortified. Now he'd have to try and do a retrospective deal with the publishers of "Big Boss Man" too. The Colonel was going to skin him alive.

"Guitar Man" and "Big Boss Man" were both minor hits for Elvis (healthy sales but no gold discs awarded). It wasn't enough to resurrect his career, but it was enough to convince a cynical media to take Elvis seriously. But "Guitar Man' wasn't just a flash in the pan. It would go on to play a significant part in the artistic rebirth of Elvis Presley, which, after five years in the doldrums, was just around the corner.

Elvis on the set of *Spinout*, 1966.
Bettmann/Corbis BE078987

Elvis in *Clambake*, 1967. Sunset Boulevard/Corbis 42-25697399

ELVIS AND PRISCILLA GET MARRIED

ABOVE: Elvis and Priscilla are pronounced man and wife by Nevada Supreme Court Justice David Zenoff on May 1, 1967, in a brief ceremony in their suite at the Aladdin Hotel in Las Vegas. The bride's sister, Michelle Beaulieu (right) served as Maid of Honor at the wedding. *Bettmann/Corbis BE020607*

RIGHT: Elvis and Priscilla sit cheek to cheek after their wedding. *Bettmann/Corbis U1553391*

LEFT: Cutting the wedding cake. *Bettmann/Corbis U1553392*

ABOVE AND TOP RIGHT: Elvis and Priscilla prepare to board a chartered aircraft after their marriage. Both: *Bettmann/Corbis U1553957-5 and BE020606*

RIGHT: Some nine months after the wedding, on February 7, 1968, Elvis, Priscilla, and Lisa Marie leave Baptist Hospital. *Bettmann/Corbis BE045752*

Chapter 16

The Comeback Special

"I'm planning a lot of changes... You can't go on doing the same thing year after year. It's been a long time since I've done anything professional, except make movies and cut albums... Before long I'm going to make some personal appearance tours... I want to see some places I've never seen before. I miss the personal contact with audiences." ~ Elvis Presley

THE COMEBACK SPECIAL

"There is something magical about watching a man who has lost himself find his way back home... He sang with the kind of power people no longer expect from rock 'n' roll singers."
~ Jon Landau's review of Elvis's 1968 TV Special

In 1968, the Colonel made a deal with NBC Television for an Elvis Christmas Special, in which he envisaged Elvis singing Christmas carols while roasting chestnuts over an open fire, dressed, no doubt, in a Santa Claus outfit. NBC weren't too keen on the idea of a Christmas special—but they couldn't turn down Elvis Presley, who hadn't done any TV work for eight long years. They hired Steve Binder to produce the show.

Binder was a hot, young producer with a music-orientated track record. He'd produced Hullabaloo, a successful, weekly, rock show that featured all the top acts of the day, most notably the Rolling Stones. He'd also produced several one-off, music specials. He'd made his name with a controversial Petula Clark show during which she, a white singer, had embraced her guest, Harry Belafonte, a black singer. Inter-racial physical contact was dynamite in a racially-polarized society, and it was greeted with howls of protest from America's self-appointed "moral" guardians, but the civil rights movement, of which Belafonte was a leading light, saw it as another step closer to the promised land.

Binder was a child of his time, preferring the Beatles and the Beach Boys to an old has-been like Elvis, but Bones Howe, Binder's veteran sound engineer, got excited. He'd worked with Elvis in 1956–57, in the good old days at Radio Recorders, when a young, uninhibited Elvis was a force of nature, sweeping all before him. As he talked, Binder started to see the possibilities. Then, suddenly, it

ABOVE AND LEFT: Elvis was resurrected as a rock 'n' roll star by his performance in the "boxing ring." *Michael Ochs Archives/Corbis 42-17853344.*

clicked. The Elvis special should be the resurrection of a legend. He would ditch the Christmas format, and show the real Elvis—Elvis the artist. He went to see Bob Finkel, the executive producer, and gave it the hard sell. Finkel loved it, but he didn't think the Colonel would agree to it. There was only one way to find out. Finkel arranged a meeting with the Colonel.

The meeting took place—at the Colonel's insistence—in his office, rather than that of NBC (don't go crawling to them…make them come crawling to you). He also insisted that the meeting begin at seven o'clock in the morning (another favorite tactic—get 'em before they're properly awake). On the appointed day, just before seven, a three-

BELOW: Bones Howe. *Michael Ochs Archives/Getty Images 74276130*

man delegation from NBC arrived at the Colonel's offices, the heart of the Presley empire.

Bob Finkel, Steve Binder, and Bones Howe were well prepared. They'd marshaled and rehearsed their arguments, they'd psyched themselves up, and they were ready to lock horns with the Colonel. The Colonel, brimming with bonhomie, let them in. The Colonel's office was a shrine to Elvis. It was jam-packed with Elvis memorabilia, Elvis merchandising and Elvis promotional material. All the walls, from floor to ceiling, were covered with photographs of Elvis.

Everywhere they looked they saw hundreds of photographs of Elvis, some giant, some small, some grinning, some surly, looking back at them. The Colonel's huge desk was piled high with stacks of Elvis promotional material, and, on the wall behind it, was a picture gallery of memorable moments in the Colonel's life; the Colonel with Lyndon Johnson, the Colonel with Bob Hope, the Colonel with Frank Sinatra and a large photograph of the Colonel dressed up as a snowman at a charity event.

To the side was a strategically half-open door revealing the shipping department which, even at seven in the morning, was a hive of activity, as the Colonel's dedicated workers toiled ceaselessly, dispatching the latest Elvis merchandise to the four corners of the civilised world. It was meant to impress, and it did.

But the Colonel wasn't finished. The meeting, he said, would be held in the conference hall. He led them through a maze of corridors, decorated every few yards by an Elvis gold disc. Finally, the Colonel showed them into the "conference hall." It was a huge, high-ceilinged kitchen/canteen. A long table ran the full length of the room. At one end of the table was a heavy, straight-backed, throne-like chair. While they helped themselves to coffee, the Colonel sat on the throne and waited for his guests to join him. "He looked like the Wizard of Oz," recalls Bones Howe.

Once seated, Bob Finkel, still psyched up, cut to the chase. How would the Colonel feel about ditching the Christmas format and replacing it with a show that would celebrate Elvis the artist, Elvis the performer, Elvis the King of Rock 'n' Roll?

He waited for a response, but the Colonel wasn't ready to talk business. Instead, for almost an hour, he held court, regaling them with stories from his colorful past. He talked about his time as a carnival huckster, detailing the scams he'd been involved in and the shady, but lucrative, deals he'd cut. He talked about his days in country music when he'd managed several stars, including Eddy Arnold who became, thanks to the Colonel's astute management, the biggest name for nearly a decade.

And then he talked about Elvis and all the astronomic deals he'd cut with the Hollywood sharks, who'd seriously underestimated him. He was a born raconteur, and the stories were peppered with good ol' boy humor, but the subtext was clear. The Colonel was not to be taken lightly, and you did so at your peril. He was the ringmaster, the eminence grise, the biggest beast in the jungle, and he'd outwitted far better men than anybody NBC could find to represent them.

The NBC delegation found the Colonel's stories fascinating, offering, as they did, a glimpse into the dark chambers of a manipulative mind that made Machiavelli seem like an innocent abroad. Then, suddenly, the Colonel was talking about the show.

"We don't care what material you submit for the show," he was saying. "If Mr Presley likes it, Mr Presley will do it. However, Mr Presley must be the publisher of the material, or else we must communicate with the publisher and arrangements must be made.

"We're not going to tell you boys what to do creatively," the Colonel continued, "because that's what we hired you for. But if you step out of line, we're going to let you know it." The threat was followed by a palliative. "You guys are going to have a million-dollar experience," he said.

The meeting broke up and the Colonel shepherded them out of the building. Just before saying goodbye, almost as an afterthought, the Colonel said only one thing was non-negotiable. The last song in the show had to be a Christmas song.

Back out on the street, the NBC delegation couldn't believe their good fortune. They'd got nearly everything they wanted without even trying. The truth was that Elvis

ABOVE: *Frank Carroll/Sygma/Corbis 42-15964847*

himself wasn't too keen on the Christmas format and had hinted to the Colonel that he'd like to do something more meaningful. He was fed up of sleepwalking through stupid films singing stupid songs.

The Colonel, one of nature's great vulgarians, didn't understand artistic integrity, but he got the message. So, rather than admit that the Christmas format was a lousy idea, he presented his retreat as an act of noblesse oblige. His insistence on the last song in the show being a Christmas song might just have been the Colonel leaving a little grit in the oyster. The Colonel giveth, and the Colonel taketh away.

Elvis was so enthusiastic about recording the show he

the dressing room but he didn't fancy trying to sell that to the Colonel.

The jam session would be the only live segment. The rest would be pre-recorded, including Elvis's vocals, so he'd be lip-synching for most of the show. Songs had to be selected, arrangements and orchestrations had to be written, musicians had to be hired and rehearsed, dancers had to be choreographed and the nearest takeaway pizza outlet experienced an economic boom.

Binder was a canny operator, making sure that Elvis was involved at every stage of the process and consulted frequently. As a result, Elvis appeared to be in a state of grace, always unfailingly polite and brimming with commitment to the enterprise. This show could be his salvation. He wasn't going to sleepwalk through this.

Binder decided that the show would be loosely based on Elvis's rise to fame, using the Jerry Reed song "Guitar Man" as a running motif. The song had been a recent mini-hit for Elvis and seemed to suggest that he wasn't quite as artistically dead as he appeared to be.

On the first day of recording, Elvis, consumed by nerves, tried to back out of the jam-session segment. He wasn't worried about the musical side of things but, without a script, he was afraid his ad-libs would dry up. Binder put his foot down. It was, he said, too late to back out. They'd been given prompt-sheets suggesting stories to tell and ad-libs that would be jumping-off points so, he said, just go out there and enjoy it. Still, Elvis wasn't convinced. But Binder was.

"Even if you only go out there, sit down, look at everyone, get up, and walk off, then that's fine," he said evenly. "But you are going out there."

The set for the jam sessions was called the "boxing ring" because the similarly sized square podium upon which the musicians would be surrounded by a small crowd of about 200 pretty girls, hand-picked by the Colonel, who made sure the prettiest were right at the front, gazing up adoringly at his boy.

They sat on chairs arranged in a circle. Scotty Moore sat to his immediate left, playing electric guitar, and DJ sat directly in front of him, playing on a guitar case. Charlie

moved into the TV studios for the duration. NBC moved a piano and a bed into their most spacious dressing room and he settled in. Always in attendance were the Memphis Mafia, who were there when he woke up and only left when he went to bed.

While Elvis rehearsed the show they waited in his dressing room. When Elvis knocked off for the day, he'd return to the dressing room where they'd get their guitars out and sing their favorite songs deep into the night. Binder heard them playing and thought it was better than the music they were rehearsing. He loved the raw spontaneity and the raucous banter.

Then he had "the big idea." They would open the show with a jam session. Elvis, accompanied by, say, Scotty Moore and DJ Fontana, would sing his Rock 'n' Roll classics, interspersed with banter about the old days. For a while, he seriously considered shooting the whole show in

Hodge sat to his right, playing acoustic guitar and Alan Fortas, one of the Memphis Mafia who wasn't even a musician, played tambourine. Lance LeGault, Elvis's film double, sat on the rostrum behind him, also playing tambourine. Elvis was playing his blonde Gibson J200 acoustic.

Elvis looked magnificent. He was lean, fit and tanned and his raven-black hair, set off by the first set of sideburns he'd grown for a decade, glinted under the studio lights. The only thing that jarred was the black leather outfit he was wearing.

Anyone with the vaguest sense of "cool" knows that black leather outfits only work if they stay close to the biker ethos, but NBC's wardrobe department, ignorant of this fact, took all the motorcycle out of it and the resulting ensemble looked, from certain angles, like a black leather Babygro. It didn't hang right, it didn't move when he did and it looked uncomfortable. But once they started the first song it didn't seem to matter.

They kicked off with "That's All Right (Mama)." It was a little ragged but all the old magic was still there. Then came "Heartbreak Hotel." Elvis messed the words up, but laughed it off. The next song was "Love Me," which he sang with mock sensuality. Then Elvis screwed it up. He swapped guitars with Scotty, who looked mortified. Now Elvis was playing rhythm on an amplified guitar, drowning out Scotty, playing his signature licks on Elvis's acoustic. It changed the balance of the music, robbing it of its subtlety and much of its character. Elvis carried the set through sheer force of personality, but something crucial had been lost.

When the session was over, Elvis stayed on the boxing ring. The band left and Elvis sang a song, backed by an off-screen orchestra. He sang "Memories," a turgid ballad beloved of a million cabaret crooners, and the mood of expectation was instantly dissipated.

And that was the end of the first day's shoot. Binder was ecstatic, believing he'd captured the real Elvis on camera. And, to a degree, he had. It was better than anything Elvis had done since the Army but it wasn't as good as it could have been. When, the following Christmas, the TV Special was aired, this section was

ABOVE, LEFT, AND OVERLEAF: *Frank Carroll/Sygma/Corbis 42-15964843/-44, and 42-15964998; Redferns/Getty Images 85240807*

universally hailed as a rebirth, the dawn of a new age, a watershed in the career of Elvis Presley. And nobody mentioned the guitar swap.

The following day, Binder and Elvis were summoned to the Colonel's office. Binder was looking forward to it, because he'd never seen Elvis and the Colonel together. He

146

was intrigued. When they arrived, the Colonel was making a personal phone call, so they waited in the outer office. The secretary's intercom crackled to life. It was the Colonel.

"Send in Elvis and Bindle please," he said. The Colonel had adopted the habit of wilfully mispronouncing Binder's name, as if he couldn't be bothered to remember the name of a mere functionary.

As they walked into the Colonel's office Binder noticed a change in Elvis's body language. "Immediately, a whole physical thing happened," he recalls. "He was standing there, sort of like a child, with his hands crossed in front of his crotch and his head bowed."

"It's been called to my attention," said the Colonel, "that there's no Christmas song in this special, and, Bindle, Elvis wants a Christmas song in the special. Isn't that right, Elvis?"

"Yes, sir," mumbled Elvis, without looking up.

Binder couldn't believe what he was hearing. He looked over at Elvis, who was shuffling uncomfortably, still avoiding eye contact. Binder turned to the Colonel.

"Look," he said. "If Elvis wants a f**king Christmas song in the special, we'll put a f**king Christmas song in the special."

Then, the Colonel, having established supremacy, abruptly dismissed them. No sooner had they left the building, and out of earshot of the two hired thugs from the William Morris Agency who were guarding the Colonel, Elvis gleefully elbowed Binder in the ribs.

"F**k him," he said.

Binder took him at his word and continued the search for an alternative song with which to end the show. He was looking for a song that would sum up Elvis's life. A mission statement for all to hear. If he couldn't find one, they might yet have to end the show with a f**king Christmas song.

After the excitement of the live section, the rest of the show was a disappointment. Whenever Elvis sang a song, he was surrounded by mini-skirted go-go dancers who wouldn't have been out of place in one of the tedious, conveyer-belt films from which he was trying to escape. Even the "Guitar Man" section was squandered thanks to

ham-fisted band arrangements that were inappropriate and cumbersome.

Then, suddenly, there was only one day's shooting left and Binder still didn't have a closing song. With the Christmas song looming over his head like the Sword of Damocles, he tried a last desperate throw of his dice. He approached Earl Brown, the show's vocal arranger, and asked him to write a song that summed up Elvis's life. Overnight. Brown spent the night writing and, by the morning, had a song called "If I Can Dream." He played it to Binder, who loved it, so he got Brown to play it for Elvis.

The song is a turgid power ballad with trite, aspirational lyrics, but Elvis loved it (Sam Phillips would have laughed it out of the studio). They informed the Colonel who, as expected, resisted the change, but when Elvis, in a rare moment of assertiveness, insisted that "If I Can Dream" should close the show, the Colonel had no choice but to capitulate. Binder, finally, had his ending.

In dramatic lighting, Elvis sang the song as if it were the last song he would ever sing. He threw everything into it with a desperate intensity that gave the song an emotional punch it otherwise lacked.

And that was it. Everybody involved was euphoric. The show had been an unqualified success. Even the Colonel seemed moderately satisfied. Elvis considered the show a turning point in his career. He told the Colonel he was finished with Hollywood and wanted to start gigging again. "I never want to do another film I don't like," he said, "and I never want to sing another song I don't like."

When, the following Christmas, the show was networked, it was greeted, by audiences and critics alike, with universal acclaim. After nearly a decade in the artistic wilderness, Elvis was back.

Now it was up to the Colonel to come up with some quality gigs. The obvious choice, often hinted at by Elvis in press interviews, was a world tour. Elvis had never performed outside America and there was a neglected, global audience hungry for their first sight of Elvis in the flesh. Instead, the Colonel booked him into a month-long residency at the International Hotel in Las Vegas.

Chapter 17

The Memphis Mafia

"I know I drove all those other guys [the other members of the Mafia] crazy buying you this house, but your mother died when you were a year old, and you never had a home, and I wanted to be the one to give it to you." ~ **Elvis to Jerry Schilling when he gave him a house as wedding gift**

LEFT: Elvis and "the Memphis Mafia" hold out their badges of office as honorary deputy sheriffs of Shelby County, Tennessee. *Frank Carroll/Sygma/Corbis 42-15964847*

THE MEMPHIS MAFIA

"There are too many people that depend on me. I'm too obligated. I'm in too far to get out." ~ Elvis Presley

As the 1960s ended and a new decade began, it was apparent Elvis had become the victim of his appetites and the prisoner of his desires. His every whim, however outlandish, had to be indulged immediately. He was prone to impulsive shopping sprees, buying expensive gifts for those he considered his closest friends. Favorite purchases were jewelry, guns, and cars.

Sol Schwarz, his personal jeweler, even went out on the road with the band just in case Elvis felt the need to buy a piece of jewelry at four o'clock in the morning. At other times he was subject to regular visits. Unannounced, Elvis would arrive at his shop and pick out any items of jewelry that took his fancy, sometimes spending $30,000 per visit. "He was like a kid in a candy shop," recalls Schwarz.

Sometimes, on a whim, he would trawl the local gun shops to buy assorted firearms for the Memphis Mafia, who stored them with the armoury of guns he'd already bought them on previous shopping sprees, during which again he rarely spent less than $30,000. As a result, the Memphis Mafia accumulated more firepower than the Sicilian originators.

Vernon, in charge of the purse strings, was appalled. His boy was starting to make a serious dent in his personal fortune. It was time for a little fatherly advice. He took Elvis aside and outlined his concerns. If Elvis continued to spend money at his present rate, he'd soon be bankrupt. He had to stop buying expensive gifts for all and sundry, particularly the Memphis Mafia, who were already paid very well for doing nothing. "You can't buy friendship," he sagely said.

As he poured out his worries, he got more and more

agitated and Elvis, touched by the old man's obvious concern for his son's welfare, sought to lighten his burden.

"Don't worry, Daddy," said Elvis, going on to explain that he was only spending a tiny fraction of his total wealth, so there was no need to worry. Elvis Presley Enterprises was not going to run out of money. Vernon wasn't convinced or placated.

Elvis, touched by the old man's concern for his welfare, sought to lighten his burden. There must be a way to bring a smile back to his father's face. After some thought, he came up with the perfect solution. The following morning, when Vernon came down for breakfast, a grinning Elvis handed him a set of car keys and led him outside. There, parked on the Graceland forecourt, was a brand-new, top-of-the-range Mercedes, gleaming in the sun.

"It's all yours," said Elvis, waving in the general direction of the car. Vernon, shoulders slumped, said nothing. Elvis, ploughing on regardless, pointed out all the features of the car. Still Vernon said nothing. Elvis, seeking some response, offered one final recommendation. The Mercedes, he said, was exactly the same model he'd bought for Charlie Hodge only yesterday.

Vernon was at the end of his tether. It was time to bring in the big guns. He spoke to Priscilla, whom he knew was also getting seriously worried. Elvis might brush off Vernon's concerns but knowing that Priscilla shared them would surely convince him of the seriousness of the situation. They decided to enlist the help of the Colonel. The Colonel, it transpired, was also concerned about Elvis's profligacy, so, he said, they had his unequivocal support.

Vernon suggested that they confront Elvis directly. If the three people closest to him couldn't make him see the error of his ways, then nobody could. So, if the Colonel came over to Graceland the following day, there would be plenty of chances to steer Elvis off to somewhere private and have a quiet word. The Colonel agreed.

But, the following morning, the Colonel phoned to say that, due to some crisis or other, he wouldn't be able to attend. He suggested they go ahead without him, but make it clear to Elvis that he was in broad agreement. So, armed

ABOVE AND LEFT: Elvis Presley at the wedding of his bodyguard Sonny West and Judy Morgan, on December 28, 1971.
Frank Carroll/Sygma/Corbis 42-18287709 and -10

Elvis and Priscilla attend the wedding of his old friend George Klein and Barbara Sally Head, January 1970. *Frank Carroll/Sygma/Corbis rv15656-14*

with the Colonel's seal of approval, Vernon and Priscilla took Elvis to one side and talked frankly.

Elvis listened in silence as they pleaded with him to cut down on his spending. He had to stop buying expensive gifts for everybody, particularly the do-nothing Memphis Mafia, who were already armed to the teeth, weighed down by expensive jewelry, and driving around in flash cars. They didn't want to stop Elvis spending money, they just wanted him to spend it more wisely. And less of it. "There have to be some checks and balances," said Vernon.

Elvis, fighting to control his rising anger, explained to them that it was his money and he'd spend it any way he damn well pleased. He reminded them that they owed their privileged lifestyle to the fruits of his labour and, consequently, had no say in the matter. He was looking forward to telling the Colonel about all this, he said, because the Colonel enjoyed a good laugh.

Vernon said that the Colonel agreed with them and would have been present were it not for a cast-iron alibi. Elvis erupted. "The Colonel agreed?' he shouted. "Well, f**k the Colonel."

He turned on his heel, walked out of the mansion, got in the nearest car and drove off. Vernon and Priscilla were shaken. It hadn't gone quite as they'd imagined. They thought that, this time, they just might have gone too far. They weren't worried that he'd stormed off in a black mood because it wasn't the first time it had happened. He'd always drive around for a couple of hours, calm down, get bored, and then, rather sheepishly, come home. But this time he didn't.

As time passed, they started phoning around the people with whom he might have taken refuge. No one had seen him. They knew it would be a fruitless exercise because even if Elvis had been with them, he would have sworn them to secrecy.

Over the next few days, Graceland was on red alert. If the phone rang, it was answered quickly, while everybody within earshot held their breath, hoping it was the boss. But it never was. He seemed to have disappeared off the face of the earth.

ABOVE: Elvis at the Hilton Hotel, New York on June 9, 1972, with his bodyguards. *Tom Wargacki/WireImage /Getty Images 75428050*

Chapter 18

The King Meets the President

"I am Elvis Presley and I admire you and have great respect for your office." ~ **Elvis Presley**

ABOVE AND PAGE 157: President Richard Nixon meets Elvis at the White House. *National Archive/Newsmakers/ Getty Images 1445200* and *Corbis NA012822.*

THE KING MEETS THE PRESIDENT

"It was a pleasure to meet with you in my office recently."
~ Richard Nixon

The story so far: Elvis had gone missing in December 1970, causing consternation among the Memphis Mafia. Then one night, Jerry Schilling, one of Elvis's most trusted lieutenants, was relaxing in his flat in Los Angeles when the phone rang. He answered it.

"It's me," said a familiar voice. First, Elvis swore Schilling to secrecy, then told him that he was in Washington Airport just about to fly to see him. He'd already phoned Gerald Peters, his new limousine driver who also lived in Los Angeles, to meet him at the airport, and asked him to bring along $500 because he didn't have any ready cash. If Schilling could meet him at the airport, Peters could drive them both back to Schilling's flat where he could lay low for a few days.

When Schilling saw Elvis, he was shocked. He had no luggage, his clothes were dishevelled, his eyes were bloodshot, his face was alarmingly puffed up and he was eating a bar of chocolate. At first, Schilling thought he'd been in a fight, but there were no bruises and no cuts. Gerald Peters—a tall, imposing Englishman whom Elvis called "Sir Gerald," was a professional chauffeur who had once been Winston Churchill's long-term driver—dropped them off at Schilling's flat. Without being asked, he placed himself at Elvis's disposal, night or day.

Schilling was worried about Elvis's swollen face, so, as soon as they got inside his flat, he suggested calling a doctor. Elvis brushed the idea aside, claiming the swelling was an allergic reaction to a new drug he'd been taking.

But Schilling insisted and Elvis finally relented. While they waited for the doctor to arrive, Elvis produced another bar of chocolate and wolfed it down.

As soon as the doctor entered the flat he was sworn to secrecy. The doctor huffily declared that all doctor/patient relationships were confidential. The doctor examined Elvis. Schilling stayed in the room while he did so because he was afraid that Elvis, if left alone, might offer the doctor a huge amount of money for some prescription drug he'd been intending to try. The doctor delivered his prognosis. He couldn't be sure but he thought the facial puffiness was due to a food allergy of some sort, probably chocolate. Schilling paid him and he left.

Alone again with Elvis, Schilling tried to find out what Elvis had been doing during his absence. "Why did you go to Washington?" he asked. Because, said Elvis, it had been the destination of the first flight out of Memphis. He didn't care where it was going, he just wanted to be someplace else. But, he added, he was going back to Washington tomorrow because he had some unfinished business to take care of, and he wanted Schilling to come with him. Schilling asked why, but Elvis wouldn't tell him.

Schilling had some prior commitments and could only come for a couple of days, so Elvis phoned another Memphis Mafioso, Sonny West (Red's brother), who was living in Memphis, as back-up. He told him that he and Schilling were going to Washington and wanted him to come too, just in case his business lasted longer than two days. West agreed, but asked if he could ring Vernon and Priscilla, because they were sick with worry. Elvis agreed, but only on condition that West didn't tell them where he was, or what he was doing. All he could tell them was that he was all right. Then, after eating another couple of bars of chocolate, he went to bed.

The following day, they caught the midnight flight from LA to Washington. The flight was unusual, to say the least. It began when Elvis met some GIs on their way home from Vietnam. Impulsively, he gave them the $500 Gerald Peters had given him. Then he discovered that George Murphy, the Republican Senator for California, was on board, and off he went to find him. When he got back to his seat, he was consumed by patriotic fervor. He wanted to write a letter, he told Schilling, and he asked a passing stewardess for pen and paper. When she brought them, Elvis spent the rest of the flight writing a six-page letter on American

Airlines stationary. When he'd finished, he handed the letter to Schilling, asking for his opinion.

Schilling was startled to discover that it was addressed to Richard Nixon. The letter started:

Dear Mr President,
First I would like to introduce myself. I am Elvis Presley and admire you and Have Great Respect for your office. I talked to Vice President Agnew in Palm Springs three weeks ago and expressed my concern for our country. The Drug Culture, the Hippy Elements, the SDS, Black Panthers, etc. do not consider me as their enemy or as they call it The Establishment. I call it America and I love it. Sir I can and will be of any service that I can to help the country out. I wish not to be given a title or an appointed position. I can and will do more good if I were made a Federal agent at Large, and I will help but by doing it my

way through my communications with people of all ages. First and foremost I am an entertainer but all I need is the Federal credentials. I have done an in-depth study of Drug Abuse and Communist Brainwashing Techniques and I am in the middle of the whole thing, where I can do the most good. I am Glad to help just so long as it is kept very Private…

The letter rambled on about the dangers facing America, but always returned to the same point. That America would be safer if he, Elvis, were appointed a card-carrying agent for the BNDD (the Bureau of Narcotics and Dangerous Drugs). He finished by telling the President that he had a special gift for him (it was a chrome-plated, World War II Navy Colt revolver).

After reading the letter, Schilling was convinced that Elvis had finally lost the plot. Here was the most popular entertainer in America offering to snitch on his devoted fans. Then, it clicked. Elvis just wanted a BNDD official Federal Agent badge.

Elvis had a huge collection of police badges. Wherever he played a gig, he was always guarded by the local police department, so there were always clusters of police loitering in the backstage area. Elvis was drawn to them because he loved their hair-raising stories of derring-do. The policemen, flattered by the King of Rock 'n' Roll's attention, always offered him an honorary local police badge, which he accepted, but he wanted more. He didn't want an honorary police badge, he wanted a real police badge. Impossible, they said, because real police badges were only issued to bona-fide law enforcement officers and it was illegal for a civilian to possess one.

Just supposing he wanted to buy one, Elvis would ask—hypothetically, of course—how much would it cost? The police—speaking hypothetically, of course—would name a price. And Elvis had his real police badge.

Collecting badges soon became an obsession, compounded when his lawyer introduced him to John O'Grady, a private detective who had once been the head of the Los Angeles Narcotics Department. O'Grady, who claimed to have conducted over 500 drug busts, was an

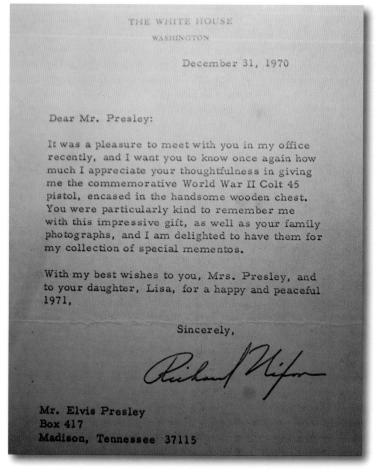

ABOVE: A letter from President Nixon to Elvis following the meeting. *Mario Tama/Getty Images 1429607*

RIGHT: Elvis pushed for a BNDD badge at his meeting with Nixon. This one is from the Bureau of Drug Abuse Control that was merged with the Federal Bureau of Narcotics to form the BNDD. *Matthew Polak/Sygma/Corbis 0000310729-016*

abrasive character with extreme reactionary views who told Elvis that Colonel Parker was a "rude, crude son-of-a-bitch" and told him to sack Schilling—whom he'd overheard expressing liberal views—because he suspected him of being a Communist.

During one of their frequent conversations, O'Grady proudly showed Elvis his BNDD Federal Agent badge, awarded in recognition of his undercover activities. Sensing that O'Grady wouldn't sell his badge for any price, Elvis was determined to get one of his own, and often talked about it to anybody who would listen.

That was what all this was about, thought Schilling. Elvis had worked out how to get a BNDD badge—ask the President of the United States of America to award him one, in return for which Elvis, the most recognisable man on the planet, would go undercover among his own fans seeking out drug-abusing, hippy-loving Commies.

They arrived in Washington in the early hours and took a cab to the hotel, stopping off at the White House to drop the letter off. At 6.30 in the morning, Elvis handed the letter to a uniformed guard at the gate. At first, the guard didn't recognize Elvis, but when he did he went out of his way to be helpful, promising to deliver the letter personally. Elvis thanked him, gave him his autograph and a bar of chocolate and got back in the cab.

As soon as they'd checked into their rooms, Schilling insisted that they call a doctor because Elvis's face was still puffed-up. Elvis reluctantly agreed. After giving Elvis a thorough examination, the Doctor offered Elvis his advice: Elvis would be fine, he said, if he stopped eating chocolate. His duty discharged, Schilling went to bed. He'd only been asleep for about an hour when he was woken by a knock on the door. It was Elvis.

He was dressed in a black suit with a brass-buttoned, Napoleonic jacket worn like a cape and a white high-collared shirt, open at the neck, revealing two chunky gold pendants. The outfit was set off by a belt with a huge gold buckle and he was wearing rhinestone-encrusted, wrap-around sunglasses.

He looked like he was just about to go onstage. He was, he said, going over to the Bureau of Narcotics and Dangerous Drugs, where he was expected, because Senator Murphy—the guy on the plane—had told him that he would use his connections to fix up a meeting with the

director, John Ingersoll, and he'd hired a limousine for the day to take him there. Oh, and if President Nixon rang, Jerry should tell him that he could be contacted at the Bureau. Schilling, musing on the surreality of life, went back to bed.

He was woken by the telephone ringing. He picked up the receiver, half-expecting it to be President Nixon. It wasn't the President, but it was the White House. The voice introduced itself as Bud Krogh, deputy counsel to the President. He'd received Mr Presley's letter to the President. Yes, the President could see Mr Presley. In 45 minutes' time? Schilling was stunned. What had started out as an Elvis whim to be indulged had suddenly turned into cold, hard fact.

Schilling phoned the BNDD and asked to speak to Elvis Presley. He was put through to the office of John Finlator, the deputy director. Elvis came to the phone. He was in a foul mood because Finlator had just refused to give him a BNDD badge, citing all the legal reasons that made it impossible. "I'm not doing any good here," said Elvis.

Schilling told him the President had agreed to meet him, but they had to be there in forty-five minutes. Elvis said he'd pick Schilling up at the hotel and they'd go straight to the White House. By the time Elvis picked them up, Sonny West had arrived from Memphis; the trio clambered into the limousine and off they went. This was the moment Elvis had been working for, but now it was here he seemed subdued, contenting himself by playing with the chrome-plated Colt he was going to give to the President.

Elvis's letter had caused some consternation in the White House. Was it really Elvis Presley? And if it was, was it just some sort of publicity stunt? Then John Ingersoll had called to say that he had Elvis Presley loose in the Bureau. Bud Krogh, uncertain of what to do, needed the advice of a higher authority, so he called his boss, White House Chief of Staff Bob Haldeman, and explained the delicate situation.

"You must be kidding," said Haldeman, but authorized the visit because he thought Elvis might be interested in taking part in their upcoming anti-drug publicity campaign. Celebrity endorsements were a bit thin on the ground—so far, they'd only secured the services of Jack Webb, the star of TV's *Dragnet*, and America's favorite evangelist, Billy Graham, hardly voices to influence the targeted youth of the nation—so recruiting Elvis might be something of a coup.

Bud Krogh was sitting in his office, when Bill Duncan, head of White House security rang to tell him that Mr Presley had arrived. But they had a problem. Mr Presley was carrying a gun. They'd tried to confiscate it, but Mr Presley was refusing to hand it over because it was a personal gift for the President. "You know we can't let him take a gun into the Oval Office," said Duncan.

Krogh suggested they explain that no-one, apart from the security detail, was allowed to bring firearms into the White House and offer to accept the gift on behalf of the President. This they did, and Elvis handed over the gun.

When Elvis walked into his office, flanked by Schilling and West, Krogh was stunned by his outlandish clothes, and starting to worry whether this was such a good idea, But when he talked to Elvis he was surprised by his sincerity and what seemed to be genuinely held beliefs. He was a patriot, said Elvis, who wanted to give something back to the country to which he owed so much. He was against the drug culture because it was eroding American society.

As he spoke, he kept scratching his neck. Krogh politely mentioned it, but Elvis dismissed it as just an allergy rash, and continued talking. He showed Krogh two autographed photographs he wanted to give the President, one of Priscilla and one of Lisa Marie. He also showed him selected items from his police badge collection, which he wanted to show the President.

ABOVE: One of Elvis's many Police badges—this one naming him as Chief Deputy in Shelby County, Tennessee. *Matthew Polak/Sygma/Corbis 0000310729-006*

At precisely 12.30 p.m. Krogh walked Elvis to the Oval Office, leaving Schilling and West in Krogh's office. Once alone, Schilling and West wondered whether Elvis would fix it up for them to meet the President. West was sure of one thing. "Well, if I know Elvis, he's going to ask," he said.

Krogh later said that Elvis—carrying the photographs and badges in one hand, and still wearing his sunglasses—was overwhelmed by the trappings of presidential power in the Oval Office. "He looked up at the ceiling, which had a large eagle emblazoned in the plaster. He looked down at the blue carpeting, which had another eagle centered on the Presidential seal, and eagles adorned the top of the armed services flags to the right of the President's desk. Elvis hesitantly walked towards the President, and I introduced him."

After some stilted small talk, Elvis spread his collection of police badges out on the President's desk, finally took off his sunglasses and pointed out badges of particular interest. Then he got down to business. Bud Krogh recorded the conversation when he later wrote his official report of the meeting.

"Elvis accused the Beatles of being a focal point of anti-Americanism. They'd made their money in America, then gone back to England where they fomented anti-American feeling." This caught Krogh off balance. Elvis hadn't mentioned the Beatles in his letter. Where was this leading? It led to Elvis condemning the Beatles for openly advocating the use of illegal drugs.

"The President then indicated that those who use drugs are also in the vanguard of anti-American protest. Violence, drug usage, dissent, protest all seemed to merge in generally the same group of young people. Presley indicated to the President, in a very emotional manner, that he was 'on your side.' Presley kept repeating that he wanted to be helpful, that he wanted to restore some respect for the flag, which was being lost. He mentioned that he was just a poor boy from Tennessee who had gotten a lot from his country, which in some way he wanted to repay.

"He also mentioned he has been studying Communist brainwashing and the drug culture for over ten years. He said he knew a lot about this and was accepted by the hippies. He said he could go right into a group of young people or hippies and be accepted, which he felt could be helpful to him in his drug drive. The President indicated his concern that Presley retain his credibility."

Then Elvis made a pitch for the BNDD badge. It would be helpful, he said, if he had some government accreditation that would sanction his undercover activities. Nixon seemed doubtful. "Bud," he said, "can we get him a badge?" "Well, Sir," said Krogh, trying, unsuccessfully, to read the President's mind, "if you want to give him a badge, I think we can get him one."

Elvis was overwhelmed with gratitude, put his arms around Nixon and gave him a bear hug. Krogh was surprised. "President-hugging was not, at least in my limited experience, a common occurrence in the Oval Office. It caught the President—and me—off guard."

"Well, I appreciate your willingness to help, Mr Presley," said Nixon, recovering his presidential composure and patting Elvis on the back. Elvis then gave Nixon the autographed photographs and told him that he had left a gift for him—a chrome-plated World War II pistol, no less—with security. "That's very kind of you," said Nixon.

In return for the gift, Nixon offered him a memento of his visit—a matching set of tie-pins and cuff-links embossed with the Presidential seal. And that seemed to be that. Elvis scooped up his badges still lying on the President's desk, put his sunglasses in his pocket, and moved toward the door. Nixon moved to show him out. Suddenly Elvis stopped. Would the President grant him just one more favor? Wondering what he was letting himself in for, Nixon cautiously agreed. Would the President just say hello to his two bodyguards who were waiting in Mr. Krogh's office? They were two of his closest friends and they'd get a real kick out of meeting the President. "It would mean a lot to them," said Elvis, "and me."

This threw security into a mild panic, because White House protocols stated that for every guest in the Oval Office there had to be a covering security operative, so two extra guests meant sorting out more staff. Nixon waved them aside. Yes, he said, of course he'd say hello to Elvis's friends. Krogh went to fetch them. Jerry Schilling and Sonny West—two good ol' boys from Memphis—suddenly found themselves being ushered into the Oval Office where Elvis Presley introduced them to the President of the United States of America.

"You've got a couple of big ones here," said Nixon, shaking their hands. "It looks like Elvis is in good hands with you two guys."

"And they're interested in helping out, too," said Elvis. Nixon then handed them each a set of tie-pins and cufflinks.

"You know, they've got wives, too," said Elvis. So, Jerry Schilling and Sonny West watched as Elvis Presley and Richard Nixon ransacked the Presidential desk-drawers looking for suitable mementoes for their wives. "He was really proud that he had set this thing up so Sonny and I could meet the President," said Schilling.

As they left the Oval Office, Krogh suggested they get something to eat at the White House mess, after which he would take them on a guided tour. Elvis caused a stir in the White House mess. "Staff members, accustomed to seeing heads of state, athletic champions and movie stars, just gaped," remembers Krogh.

The guided tour of the White House soon became a triumphant procession during which the White House staff paid homage to the King of Rock 'n' Roll. He was constantly waylaid by administrative staff, flustered typists, domestic staff, gardeners, and rest-room cleaners, all wanting his autograph. Elvis was in his element.

After the tour, they went back to Krogh's office to wait for the Bureau of Narcotics and Dangerous Drugs to deliver Elvis's BNDD badge. With delicious irony, it was delivered by deputy director John Finlator, the man who, earlier in the day, had refused to give him one. Then Elvis, his mission accomplished, thanked Bud Krogh for all his help and left the building, clutching his precious BNDD badge.

For Jerry Schilling and Sonny West, it had been just another day at the office.

Chapter 19

Viva Las Vegas?

"There are several unbelievable things about Elvis, but the most incredible is his staying power in a world where meteoric careers fade like shooting stars." ~ *Newsweek* **magazine August 11, 1969, review of Elvis's Las Vegas engagement**

LEFT: *Bettmann/Corbis U1898316*

VIVA LAS VEGAS?

"When you think of Vegas, you think of Elvis; you think of show business; you think of flash. You think of those performances."
~ Beyonce

Elvis's first album after the Comeback Special was crucial. If it failed to capitalise on the momentum generated by the TV show it would be a chance squandered, signaling a return to the doldrums. The crucial album was scheduled to be recorded at RCA Studios in LA, but there was a faction of the Memphis Mafia who were trying to persuade Elvis to record the next album at American Studios, located just a short drive from Graceland in a seedy district of South Memphis.

American was founded and run by Chips Moman, a hotshot producer who didn't suffer fools gladly. Set up in 1965, it had a fearsome reputation, having produced an unbroken string of hits for, among others, Dionne Warwick, Wilson Pickett, Neil Diamond, and Dusty Springfield. Using a subtle blend of subliminal hints and outright brainwashing, the faction convinced Elvis that not only was it a good idea but he'd thought of it in the first place. The Colonel didn't like it but, by then, Elvis was committed. Ten consecutive nights were booked at American Studios.

LEFT: Mac Davis, Steve Tyrell, and Chips Moman. *Michael Ochs Archives/Getty Images 80808645*

RIGHT: Built in 1969 by Kirk Kerkorian, the International Hotel was where Elvis started his Las Vegas residency. *Reuters/Corbis 3239310*

On the evening of Monday January 13, 1969, Elvis, suffering from a heavy cold, walked into American, and went to work. The regular studio musicians, all experienced Memphis session men, weren't easily impressed. "Of course we were thrilled about working with Elvis," said trumpet-player Wayne Jackson, "but it wasn't like doing Neil Diamond."

But when Elvis started singing, they grudgingly admitted to each other that he was something else. They were impressed by his work ethic and the strength of his voice which, despite the heavy cold, never lost either power or quality during a twelve-hour session. In fact, the worse his cold got, the better he sang. They were also astonished that when Elvis recorded a vocal, he gave a total performance with all the gyrations he employed in his stage act. He had a towel draped around his shoulders and used it to wipe himself down between takes. "He just got into it," said Mike Leech, a watching studio arranger.

For the first couple of nights, Chips Moman took a back seat, allowing Elvis and the musicians to get used to each other, but then he started to get involved. "I'm a stubborn kinda fella," he often said, "I guess I believe in what I do, so I think if a guy is hiring me to do a job I believe that's what he's hiring me to do."

Moman had an unique approach to producing. If he didn't like a song Elvis selected, then he would excuse himself and leave, only returning when Elvis selected a song that he did like. But when he did like a song, a song that was worth his time, he was galvanised. Blessed with a laconic manner, he orchestrated the session, urging Elvis and the band on to ever greater heights and, in the process, fusing them into a single recordable entity. Elvis liked him, trusted his judgement and enthusiastically followed his advice whenever it was offered.

Elvis's favored songwriter at the time was Mac Davis. He'd already recorded two of his songs, "A Little Less Conversation" for one of his forgettable films, and "Memories" for the TV Comeback Special. Davis had sent him a seventeen-track demo album, on which was "In The Ghetto," a political song drawing attention to the injustice suffered by those scraping out a meagre existence at the bottom of American society. Elvis instinctively avoided "message" songs, believing they alienated as many people as they convinced, but he loved the song so he recorded it. He sang it with magisterial authority, investing the lyric with an understated sincerity that pulled the listener into the song.

It took twenty-three takes before Elvis was satisfied. "That's a hit record," he said to nobody in particular, after he'd selected the final take. "Oh, my God, that's wonderful. This is it!" said a mesmerized Wayne Jackson—although not, presumably, as good as Neil Diamond.

The last song they recorded was the highlight of the whole ten days. It was four o'clock in the morning on the last night, and they wanted to do one more song. They tried out a few, but nothing caught fire, when Chips suggested they tried "Suspicious Minds," a song written by staff writer Mark James. A year ago, James had recorded it himself and, released as a single, it had flopped. Chips

FROM ELVIS IN MEMPHIS

RELEASED: June 17, 1969
RECORDED: January–February 1969
LENGTH: 36:42
LABEL: RCA Records
PRODUCER: Chips Moman, Felton Jarvis

Side One
1. Wearin' That Loved On Look *Dallas Frazier and A.L. Owens*
2. Only The Strong Survive *Jerry Butler, Kenny Gamble, Leon Huff*
3. I'll Hold You In My Heart (Till I Can Hold You in My Arms) *Eddy Arnold, Thomas Dilbeck, Vaughan Horton*
4. Long Black Limousine *Bobby George and Vern Stovall*
5. It Keeps Right On A-Hurtin' *Johnny Tillotson*
6. I'm Movin' On *Hank Snow*

Side Two
1. Power Of My Love *Bernie Baum, Bill Giant, Florence Kaye*
2. Gentle On My Mind *John Hartford*
3. After Loving You *Janet Lantz and Eddie Miller*
4. True Love Travels On A Gravel Road *Dallas Frazier and A.L. Owens*
5. Any Day Now *Burt Bacharach and Bob Hilliard*
6. In the Ghetto *Mac Davis*

thought he knew why. James, who had a light and insubstantial voice, just wasn't a good enough singer to deliver the dramatic punch the song required. But Elvis was.

So Chips went into overdrive. He stuck to James's original arrangement but, with Elvis at the microphone, it was almost a different song. Once again, Elvis was singing with magisterial authority, but now with the added bitterness of a man wounded and betrayed. The band, responding to his raw, emotional power, cranked up the intensity and it only needed four takes before it was in the can. Everybody agreed that it was a potential monster hit and, at seven o'clock in the morning, said their farewells and went home to bed. As he said goodbye to Chips, Elvis sought one final assurance.

"We have some hits, don't we?" he asked.

"Maybe some of your biggest," said Chips.

The resulting album was called *From Elvis In Memphis*, and "In The Ghetto" was selected as the next single. On its release, it earned him his first gold disc for four, long years. As did "Suspicious Minds" upon its release.

While Elvis had been recording the album, the Colonel had been putting the finishing touches to the Las Vegas deal. The International Hotel in Las Vegas is thirty stories high, it has 1,512 rooms, and a 2,000-capacity showroom. It was still under construction when the Colonel submitted his proposal: $500,000 for a four-week residency, one show per night, two at weekends, with Mondays off (this was in line with Frank Sinatra and Dean Martin, the highest paid acts in Vegas).

The International Hotel suggested an alternative: $400,000 for a four-week residency, two shows per night (even Frank and Dean did two shows a night) and Mondays off. They reached a compromise. Elvis would do two shows per night, but the money had to go back up to 500 grand. The International Hotel agreed, on condition that Elvis would personally conduct the opening ceremony. Signed, sealed and delivered.

Elvis didn't much like Las Vegas. It had been the scene of his greatest humiliation when, back in the days of "Elvis the Pelvis," he'd played a Las Vegas hotel. Instead of the usual sea of hysterical, teenage girls, he played to a smattering of drunken gamblers and their floozies with no interest in adolescent music. He thought of it as one of the low points in his career.

Elvis began putting a band together. He started with the guitarist. There was only one man for the job so he called Scotty Moore—but, much to his surprise, Scotty declined the offer, citing prior commitments. So he phoned James Burton, whose unmistakable guitar-playing had once lit up Ricky Nelson's records. Burton was a much-in-demand session musician, so he wasn't really interested. Besides, he had sessions already booked with John Denver and Frank Sinatra. But Elvis kept on talking. They talked for two hours, after which Burton, much to his surprise, agreed to join the band.

Elvis and Burton, who seemed to know every musician in America, put the band together. The final line-up was bass-player Jerry Scheff, keyboard-player Larry Muhoberac, rhythm guitarist John Wilkinson, and drummer Ronnie Tutt, who said that playing with Elvis was like playing with "a glorified stripper." The group was augmented by two vocal groups, the Imperials, a white, gospel group he'd already worked with, and the Sweet Inspirations, a black ensemble whose work with Aretha Franklin he'd much admired.

Add to that, an orchestra and arranger, and the total wage bill for the four-week engagement came to $80,000. The Colonel nearly had a heart attack, but if that's what Elvis wanted, then that's what Elvis got. They rehearsed for five days at RCA's Hollywood Boulevard studio. For Myrna Smith, the leader of the Sweet Inspirations, it was just another gig.

"I didn't know much about Elvis," she later said, "because that wasn't the kind of music that was played in our neighborhood. But then he walked in, looking absolutely gorgeous. He walked up to us and introduced himself, like we didn't know who he was. Then he started singing our record, so we just chimed in and fell in love with him. Rehearsals were great. He went through the whole thing, just as though he were on stage. He put so much into it, you just had to look at him."

The Colonel wasn't leaving anything to chance. Everywhere you looked in Las Vegas there was an Elvis billboard, all the local TV and radio stations were running hourly trailers for the upcoming show and he'd accumulated a mountain of promotional souvenirs, including 100,000 8x10 glossy photos of Elvis ready for distribution, all paid for by RCA. "Even the gophers in the desert will know you're here," he said to Elvis.

The opening night, July 31, was by invitation only. Among those present would be Cary Grant, Fats Domino, Paul Anka, Pat Boone, Shirley Bassey and most of the headliners from rival hotels, checking out the competition.

They had a full dress rehearsal in the afternoon, after which all Elvis had to do was wait for showtime.

"Everything was fine right up until that night,"

ABOVE: Elvis on stage for his first show in Las Vegas in 1969.
Bettmann/Corbis U1639839A LEFT: *Bettmann/Corbis U1768935*

remembers Joe Esposito. "He had no idea of how he was going to be received. He was pacing back and forth, back and forth, and you could see the sweat just pouring out of him even before he went on stage. He was always nervous before every show, but he was never nervous like that again."

He needn't have worried. When he walked, unannounced, onto the stage, the whole place erupted with joy unconfined. "Before the evening's out, I'm sure I'll have made a complete and utter fool of myself," he told the audience, "but I hope you get a kick out of watching."

Then he tore the place apart. He opened with a blistering version of "Blue Suede Shoes," and the audience couldn't believe their luck. Rock 'n' Roll classic followed Rock 'n' Roll classic, relentlessly ratcheting up the tension. The sophisticated showbiz audience started dancing on the tables, the waitresses, "visibly swooning," stopped serving, and even Cary Grant was on his feet.

After the show Elvis was euphoric. He never once lost them. He had them in the palm of his hand. His entourage, many of whom had never seen him perform live, were as stunned as the audience. Priscilla was bewitched.

"On stage, he exuded maleness, a proudness that you only see in an animal. He had this look, you know,

prowling back and forth, pacing like a tiger, and you look and you say, 'My God, this is the person that I married?' "

When the Colonel came backstage after the show, he and Elvis hugged. They didn't say anything, but when they stood back the Colonel, not given to displays of emotion, had tears in his eyes. After the post-show press conference Elvis had his photograph taken with Fats Domino who, Elvis told the watching reporters, was the real King of Rock 'n' Roll.

The delighted International Hotel booked Elvis for another residency, then another, then another. He was on the treadmill. The show deteriorated as Elvis became bored. The music was pushed into the background, replaced by showbiz inanities. One night he offered to kiss

every girl in the audience. They took him at his word and queued up at the front of the stage as he kissed every one of them while the band vamped quietly. Soon it became a nightly ritual which knocked out a good twenty minutes of the show.

He would often embark on long, rambling, stream-of-consciousness monologues that rarely made sense, and he introduced a karate section when, sometimes for ten minutes, he would go through his moves while Ronnie Tutt accentuated each move with explosive drum effects. He wasn't a musician any more, he was a circus act.

A month-long Vegas residency would be a regular feature of Elvis's live schedule in the first half of the Seventies—a decade that would bring highlights and

OPPOSITE AND ABOVE LEFT: *Bettmann/Corbis U1753544E and -44B; Sunset Boulevard/Corbis 42-25697400*

ABOVE: Elvis leaves Santa Monica California Superior Court after being granted a divorce from Priscilla on October 9, 1973. *Bettmann/Corbis*

lowlights such as his first Number 1 album for nine years, *Aloha From Hawaii Via Satellite* and an amicable divorce from Priscilla. More worryingly, his fluctuating health would necessitate a number of hospital stays. He was fighting a battle with his weight, and relying increasingly on prescription drugs. The King was still out there, but his grip on the crown was looking somewhat shaky.

Chapter 20

Elvis Leaves the Building

"This boy had everything. He had the looks, the moves, the manager, and the talent. And he didn't look like Mr. Ed like a lot of the rest of us did. In the way he looked, way he talked, way he acted – he really was different." ~ Carl Perkins

LEFT: Elvis and Elvis memorabilia has a leading position inside the Rock 'n' Roll Museum of Cleveland. *Brooks Kraft/Sygma/Corbis 42-20011823*

ELVIS LEAVES THE BUILDING

"There have been a lotta tough guys. There have been pretenders. And there have been contenders. But there is only one King."
~ Bruce Springsteen

While previous years had not been kind to the Elvis Presley legend, the public hunger for him seemed scarcely to have abated. And his standing among musicians appeared unimpeachable. Some, indeed, seemed to want to follow in the footsteps of the Beatles who had met the King by invitation in 1965, albeit in California.

Fellow artist Bruce Springsteen, the so-called "future of Rock 'n' Roll'" according to one breathless *Rolling Stone* magazine writer, had showed up in April 1976 and attempted to scale the fence of Gracelands before being escorted off the premises by security guards. Mott the Hoople's Ian Hunter had attempted to obtain entry some while earlier, while one-time Sun labelmate Jerry Lee Lewis was, more disturbingly, apprehended in November 1976 with a .38 Derringer pistol demanding to see Elvis.

As 1977 began, there were clear indications that Elvis Presley's health was in decline. He entered Memphis'

Farina Christopher/Sygma/Corbis 0000274034-001

Baptist Memorial Hospital in April and stayed for five days with intestinal flu, while a May concert in Baltimore was stopped for 30 minutes as he was attended backstage by a physician.

On June 26, 1977, he played what was to be his last gig at the Market Square Arena in Indianapolis. Five days earlier, the audience at the Rushmore Civic Center in Rapid City had witnessed a near disaster. A grossly overweight Elvis had stumbled around the stage, seemingly in a state of near-collapse. Aides waited in the wings, ready to run on and catch him should he fall.

Elvis was found slumped on the floor of a bathroom at Gracelands on the afternoon of Tuesday, August 16. He was rushed to the Baptist Memorial Hospital but declared dead on arrival. At 4 p.m., his death was announced to the world. The news came as a tremendous shock to millions of fans across the globe, and spread like wildfire. Radio and television programmes were interrupted, and across the country people stopped what they were

doing and tried to get any information they could. President Jimmy Carter paid tribute, while former president Richard Nixon, who had met Elvis in 1970, asked all Americans to fly their flags at half mast. In Memphis itself, the telephone network was jammed as many thousands of calls came flooding in.

Initial reports gave the cause of death as heart failure, and added that the cause had not been determined, although Tennessee state pathologist Dr. Jerry Francisco pointed out that no sign of drug abuse had been found. The truth was rather different—for several years before his

ABOVE LEFT: Elvis as he was in the 1970s: overweight and bejeweled. *Lynn Goldsmith/Corbis BE080852*

ABOVE: Dr. George C. Nichopoulos, Elvis's personal physician, confirmed the death at a hospital news conference late on August 16, 1977. *Bettmann/Corbis U1908928*

death, Presley had become increasingly dependent on a mixture of prescription drugs, and these, coupled with his addiction to junk food, led to his demise at the age of forty-two.

Although Elvis had carried on performing right up till his death, the young, vibrant Rock 'n' Roller that had so galvanised the nation's teenagers twenty or so years earlier had become a dim distant memory. His die-hard fans didn't seem to care, though—to them he was the

King, come what may, and through them the memory of the man who brought Rock 'n' Roll to the world would live on.

Many famous entertainers took their leave of us during 1977: opera's prima donna Maria Callas took her final curtain call in September, Charlie Chaplin, that knight of the silent screen, bowed out on Christmas morning, while easy listening champion Bing Crosby holed out after a golf match. But none of these sad losses caused the same

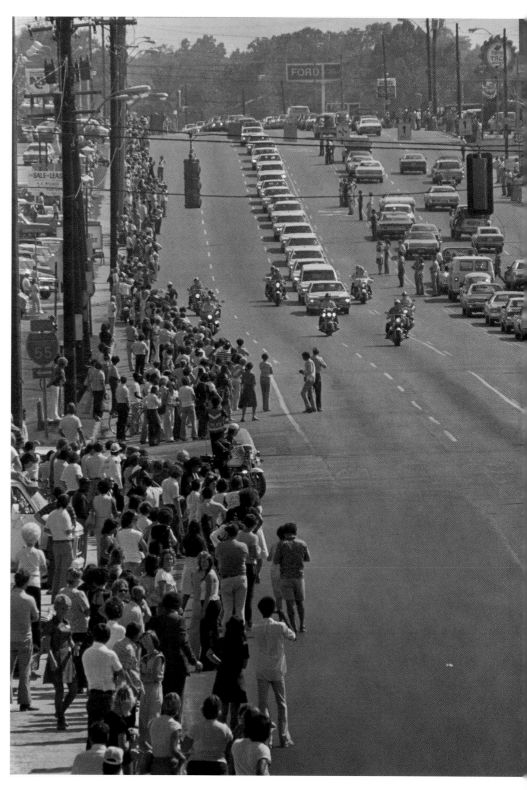

ABOVE: A crowd gathers outside the gates of Graceland for the funeral. *Shepard Sherbell/Corbis AABT002267*

RIGHT: Thousands line the streets to watch the funeral procession of August 18. *Bettmann/Corbis BE022458*

ABOVE: Medical Examiner Jerry Francisco, who signed Elvis's death certificate, confers with his attorney as he testified before the State Medical Board hearing for Dr. George Nichopoulos. Francisco testified that Presley died of heart disease. *Bettmann/Corbis U1991680*

BELOW: Graceland memorabilia. *Brooks Kraft/Sygma/Corbis 0000310088-018*

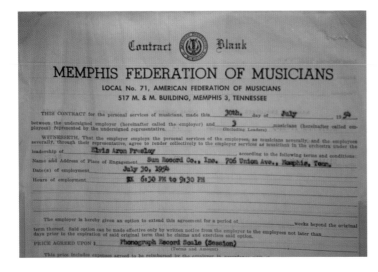

worldwide wave of sympathy and appreciation that Elvis posthumously enjoyed.

Colonel Parker, when asked about his reaction to Elvis's death said, "It's just like when he went in the army," and carried on promoting his now posthumous star. Curiously, a more heartfelt tribute came from Presley's one-time foe, Frank Sinatra. "There have been many accolades uttered about Elvis' talent and performances through the years, all of which I agree with wholeheartedly. I shall miss him dearly as a friend. He was a warm, considerate and generous man."

Elvis had left the building. His career had moved back and forth between the sublime and the ridiculous. In his prime he was simply peerless, but his two-year sabbatical gave him time to think and he returned to the world wearing a cloak of self-consciousness. It smothered his matchless talent and he could only occasionally thereafter recapture the glory days.

But that should not overshadow the achievement of those glory days. He was the most successful artist of the twentieth century. He was the template on which thousands of artists based their careers, a benchmark against which they could judge their own efforts, and is simply remembered as the King.

And the Elvis industry continues. The single "Way Down" gave him his seventeenth different UK chart-topper in 1977 in the wake of his death, while *Moody Blue*, the album on which it featured, hit the transatlantic Top Three. Eight singles and eleven albums found their way back into the UK chart.

Compilation albums have since continued to sell to new generations, particularly after the compact-disc revolution of the late 1980s. But the most exciting event occurred in June 2002 when a re-worked version of "A Little Less Conversation," a song from the soundtrack of 1968's movie *Live A Little, Love A Little*, peppered with an insistent beat added by Dutch disco remixer JXL (aka Tom Holkenborg), soared to UK Number 1.

This unexpected success not only pulled the King one place higher than the Beatles (both acts having previously registered seventeen UK chart-toppers apiece) but put him

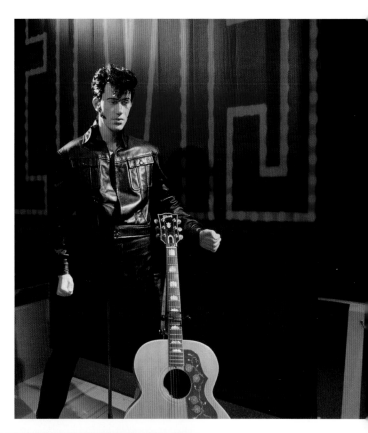

LEFT: Lisa Marie Presley appears as a guest on *The Tonight Show with Jay Leno*, May 1, 2003. *Reuters/Corbis UT0142769*

BELOW LEFT: Priscilla at the Elvis Tribute Concert of October 1994. *Neal Preston/Corbis PN010658*

RIGHT: Elvis and Elvis memorabilia has a leading position inside the Rock 'n' Roll Museum at Cleveland. *Brooks Kraft/Sygma/Corbis, 42-20011823*

BELOW: One of Elvis's cars on show. *Matthew Polak/Sygma/Corbis 0000310729-002*

up there among the Pop Star reality TV winners, not to mention the likes of Coldplay and Atomic Kitten.

There was a similar burst of activity on the seventieth anniversary of Elvis' birth when singles "Jailhouse Rock," "One Night"/"I Got Stung" and "It's Now Or Never" topped the UK chart. Admittedly the sales quantities required to achieve this once-exalted position were not what they were, but the next four months would see an impressive fourteen further titles hit the Top Five, while a new compilation album, "Love, Elvis," made Number 8.

In this era of digital downloads via the internet some early Elvis material has appeared on its seventh format— 78rpm shellac, 45rpm vinyl, album, cassette, eight-track and compact disc the others. This mind-boggling statistic surely proves that Elvis Aaron Presley will be in demand for as long as music is listened to—and by whatever means.

ABOVE: Composers/songwriters who had written for Elvis—Randy Starr, Paul Evans, Paul Parnes—and conductor/arranger George Andrews are pictured at the recording session for John Krondes and "The Elvis Hit Making Team" with the New York String Section held at Avatar Recording Studios on December 23, 2005. Elvis Presley's "Hit Team" reunited in a project to record for the first time since Elvis Presley's death. *Nancy Kaszerman/ ZUMA/Corbis 42-16191848*

Elvis Presley's star on the Walk of Fame. *Steven Vidler/Eurasia Press/Corbis 42-17963239*

ELVIS PRESLEY WEBSITE GUIDE

Your guide to some of the best Elvis-related sites on the Internet

The Official Elvis Presley website, home of Elvis Presley Enterprises (EPE):
www.elvis.com

Elvis @ Internet Movie Database (IMDb). Covers his career on the silver screen:
http://www.imdb.com/name/nm0000062/

Elvis @ Last.Fm. Listen to his greatest hits and talk with like-minded fans:
http://www.last.fm/music/Elvis+Presley

Elvis @ All Music. Handy resource with album reviews and short bio:
http://www.allmusic.com/artist/elvis-presley-p5175

Elvis Presley on MySpace:
http://www.myspace.com/thekingelvis

Elvis Presley on Facebook:
http://www.facebook.com/elvis

Elvis @ BBC. Latest BBC news and reviews:

http://www.bbc.co.uk/music/artists/01809552-4f87-45b0-afff-2c6f0730a3be

Elvis Presley Australian fansite. Founded in 1996 a handy resource:
http://www.elvispresley.com.au/

Elvis Australia. Linked to fansite, going since 1996:
http://www.elvis.com.au/

The Elvis Directory. External links and user-generated content:
http://www.elvisdirectory.co.uk/

Elvis biography with small pictures:
http://www.history-of-rock.com/elvis_presley.htm

Elvis @ The Rock 'n' Roll Hall of Fame:
http://rockhall.com/inductees/elvis-presley/

Elvis @ Yahoo Music. Music, videos, links and news:
http://new.music.yahoo.com/elvis-presley/

Elvis Presley Scrapbook. Pictures, press clippings, artefacts, downloads:
http://www.elvispresleyscrapbook.co.uk/

Elvis Presley UK Fan Club. Includes list of local branches:
http://www.elvispresleyfanclubuk.co.uk/

Elvis Presley Boulevard. Buying and selling memorabilia:
http://www.elvispresleyfanclubuk.co.uk/

Elvis unofficial fan site. Quotes, lyrics, biography:
http://elvisfansite.com/

Elvis' Sweet Sweet Spirit Fan Club (officially recognized):
http://www.elvissweetspirit.com/

Elvis Insiders Fan Club:
http://www.elvisinsiders.com

Due to the rapid turnover of internet sites we cannot guarantee all addresses will be current, but all are correct as at December 2010.

OPPOSITE, ABOVE: Elvis Presley and Barbara Eden promoting *Flaming Star* 1960. *Sunset Boulevard/Corbis 42-25697418*

OPPOSITE, BELOW: Elvis promotes *Kid Galahad*, 1962. *Sunset Boulevard/Corbis 42-25697603*

ELVIS PRESLEY FILMOGRAPHY

Film: *Love Me Tender* (1956)
Character: Clint Reno
Director: Robert D Webb
Company: 20th Century Fox
Cast: Richard Egan, Debra Paget, Neville Brand, Mildred Dunnock

Film: *Loving You* (1957)
Character: Jimmy Tompkins (Deke Rivers)
Director: Hal Kanter
Company: Paramount
Cast: Lizabeth Scott, Wendell Corey, Dolores Hart

Film: *Jailhouse Rock* (1957)
Character: Vince Everett
Director: Richard Thorpe
Company: MGM
Cast: Judy Tyler, Mickey Shaughnessy, Dean Jones

Film: *King Creole* (1958)
Character: Danny Fisher
Director: Michael Curtiz
Company: Paramount
Cast: Carolyn Jones, Walter Matthau, Dean Jagger, Dolores Hart, Vic Morrow

Film: *GI Blues* (1960)
Character: Tulsa McClean
Director: Norman Taurog
Company: Paramount
Cast: Juliet Prowse, Robert Ivers, James Douglas

Film: *Flaming Star* (1960)
Character: Pacer Burton
Director: Don Siegel
Company: 20th Century Fox
Cast: Barbara Eden, Steve Forrest, Dolores Del Rio, John McIntire

Film: *Wild In The Country* (1961)
Character: Glen Tyler
Director: Philip Dunn
Company: 20th Century Fox
Cast: Hope Lange, Tuesday Weld, Millie Perkins, John Ireland, Gary Lockwood, Christina Crawford, Rafer Johnson

Film: *Blue Hawaii* (1961)
Character: Chad Gates
Director: Norman Taurog
Company: Paramount
Cast: Joan Blackman, Angela Lansbury, Iris Adrian, Nancy Walters

Film: *Follow That Dream* (1962)
Character: Toby Kwimper
Director: Gordon Douglas
Company: United Artists
Cast: Arthur O'Connell, Anne Helm, Joanna Moore, Jack Kruschen

Film: *Kid Galahad* (1962)
Character: Walter Gulick / Dustin Holmes / Kid Galahad
Director: Phil Karlson
Company: United Artists
Cast: Gig Young, Lola Albright, Ned Glass, Joan Blackman, Charles Bronson

Film: *Girl Happy* (1965)
Character: Rusty Wells
Director: Boris Sagal
Company: MGM
Cast: Shelley Fabares, Gary Crosby, Mary Ann Mobley, Harold Stone

Film: *Tickle Me* (1965)
Character: Lonnie Beale / Panhandle Kid
Director: Norman Taurog
Company: Allied Artists
Cast: Jocelyn Lane, Julie Adams, Jack Mullaney

Film: *Harum Scarum* (1965)
Character: Johnny Tyronne
Director: Gene Nelson
Company: MGM
Cast: Mary Ann Mobley, Fran Jeffries, Michael Ansara

Film: *Girls! Girls! Girls!* (1962)
Character: Ross Carpenter
Director: Norman Taurog
Company: Paramount
Cast: Stella Stevens, Jeremy Slate

Film: *It Happened At The World's Fair* (1963)
Character: Mike Edwards
Director: Norman Taurog
Company: MGM
Cast: Joan O'Brien, Gary Lockwood, Yvonne Craig, Vicky Tiu

Film: *Fun In Acapulco* (1963)
Character: Mike Windgren
Director: Richard Thorpe
Company: Paramount
Cast: Ursula Andress, Paul Lukas, Alejandro Rey

Film: *Kissin' Cousins* (1964)
Character: Josh Morgan / Jodie Tatum
Director: Gene Nelson
Company: MGM
Cast: Arthur O'Connell, Glenda Farrell, Jack Albertson, Yvonne Craig

Film: *Viva Las Vegas* (1964)
Character: Lucky Jackson
Director: George Sidney
Company: MGM
Cast: Ann-Margret, William Demarest, Jack Carter, Nicky Blair

Film: *Roustabout* (1964)
Character: Charlie Rogers
Director: John Rich
Company: Paramount
Cast: Barbara Stanwyck, Joan Freeman, Leif Erickson, Sue Ane Langdon, Jack Albertson

Film: *Frankie And Johnny* (1966)
Character: Johnny
Director: Frederick De Cordova
Company: United Artists
Cast: Donna Douglas, Nancy Kovack, Sue Ane Langdon, Harry Morgan

Film: *Paradise, Hawaiian Style* (1966)
Character: Rick Richards
Director: D Michael Moore
Company: Paramount
Cast: James Shigeta, Suzanna Leigh

Film: *Spinout* (1966)
Character: Mike McCoy
Director: Norman Taurog
Company: MGM
Cast: Shelley Fabares, Deborah Walley, Diane McBain, Carl Betz

Film: *Easy Come, Easy Go* (1967)
Character: Lt. (JG) Ted Jackson
Director: John Rich
Company: Paramount
Cast: Dodie Marshall, Pat Priest, Pat Harrington

Film: *Double Trouble* (1967)
Character: Guy Lambert
Director: Norman Taurog
Company: MGM
Cast: Annette Day, Yvonne Romain, John Williams

Film: *Clambake* (1967)
Character: Scott Heyward / "Tom Wilson'
Director: Arthur H. Nadel
Company: United Artists
Cast: Shelley Fabares, Bill Bixby, Will Hutchins

Film: *Stay Away, Joe* (1968)
Character: Joe Lightcloud
Director: Peter Tewksbury
Company: MGM
Cast: Burgess Meredith, Joan Blondell, Katy Jurado

Film: *Speedway* (1968)
Character: Steve Grayson
Director: Norman Taurog
Company: MGM
Cast: Nancy Sinatra, Bill Bixby, Gale Gordon

Film: *Live A Little, Love A Little* (1968)
Character: Greg Nolan
Director: Norman Taurog
Company: MGM
Cast: Michele Carey, Don Porter, Dick Sargent

Film: *Charro!* (1969)
Character: Jesse Wade
Director: Charles Marquis Warren
Company: National General
Cast: Ina Balin, Victor French, Lynn Kellogg

Film: *The Trouble With Girls* (1969)
Character: Walter Hale
Director: Peter Tewksbury
Company: MGM
Cast: Marlyn Mason, Vincent Price, Sheree North, Dabney Coleman

Film: *Change Of Habit* (1969)
Character: Dr. John Carpenter
Director: William Graham
Company: Universal
Cast: Mary Tyler Moore, Barbara McNair, Ed Asner

FAR LEFT: Stella Stevens and Elvis on the set of *Girls! Girls! Girls!*, 1962. *Sunset Boulevard/Corbis 42-19502052*

LEFT: American actress Quentin Dean and Elvis in *Stay Away, Joe*, 1968. *Sunset Boulevard/Corbis 42-25697661*

ELVIS PRESLEY SELECTED DISCOGRAPHY

SINGLES

Title	US Chart	UK Chart	Year
That's All Right	-	-	1954
Blue Moon of Kentucky	-	-	1954
Good Rockin' Tonight	-	-	1954
I Don't Care If The Sun Don't Shine	74	-	1954
Milkcow Blues Boogie	-	-	1954
You're a Heartbreaker	-	-	1954
Baby, Let's Play House	-	-	1955
I'm Left, You're Right, She's Gone	-	-	1955
I Forgot To Remember To Forget	-	-	1955
Mystery Train	-	25	1955
Heartbreak Hotel	1	2	1956
I Was The One	19	-	1956
Blue Suede Shoes	20	9	1956
I Want You, I Need You, I Love You	3	14	1956
My Baby Left Me	31	-	1956
Don't Be Cruel	1	-	1956
Hound Dog	2	2	1956
Trying To Get To You	-	16	1956
Just Because	-	-	1956
Blue Moon	-	9	1956
Money Honey	76	-	1956
One-Sided Love Affair	-	-	1956
Shake, Rattle & Roll	-	-	1956
Lawdy Miss Clawdy	-	15	1956
Love Me Tender	1	11	1956
Any Way You Want Me (That's How I Will Be)	27	-	1956
Love Me	2	-	1956
When My Blue Moon Turns To Gold Again	19	-	1956
Paralyzed	59	8	1956
Old Shep	47	-	1956
Poor Boy	24	-	1956
Rip It Up	-	27	1957
Too Much	2	6	1957
Playing For Keeps	34	-	1957
All Shook Up	1	1	1957
Peace In The Valley	25	-	1957
That's When Your Heartaches Begin	58	-	1957
(Let Me Be Your) Teddy Bear	1	3	1957
Mean Woman Blues	-	-	1957
Loving You	28	24	1957
Jailhouse Rock	1	1	1957
Treat Me Nice	27		1957
(You're So Square) Baby I Don't Care	-	-	1957
Don't	1	2	1958
I Beg Of You	8	-	1958
Wear My Ring Around Your Neck	3	3	1958
Doncha Think It's Time?	21	-	1958
Hard Headed Woman	2	2	1958
Don't Ask Me Why	28	-	1958
King Creole	-	2	1958
One Night	4	1	1958
I Got Stung	8	-	1958
(Now And Then There's) A Fool Such As I	2	1	1959
I Need Your Love Tonight	4	-	1959
A Big Hunk o' Love	1	4	1959
My Wish Came True	12	-	1959
Stuck On You	1	3	1960

Title	US Chart	UK Chart	Year
Fame And Fortune	17	-	1960
It's Now Or Never	1	1	1960
A Mess Of Blues	32	2	1960
Are You Lonesome Tonight?	1	1	1960
I Gotta Know	20	-	1960
Surrender	1	1	1961
Lonely Man	32	-	1961
Flaming Star	14	-	1961
I Feel So Bad	5	4	1961
Wild In The Country	26	-	1961
(Marie's The Name) His Latest Flame	4	1	1961
Little Sister	5	-	1961
Can't Help Falling In Love	2	1	1961
Rock-A-Hula Baby	23	-	1962
Good Luck Charm	1	1	1962
Anything That's Part Of You	31	-	1962
Follow That Dream	15	34	1962
She's Not You	5	1	1962
Just Tell Her Jim Said Hello	55	-	1962
King Of The Whole Wide World	30	23	1962
Return To Sender	2	1	1962
Where Do You Come From	99	-	1962
One Broken Heart For Sale	11	12	1963
They Remind Me Too Much Of You	53	-	1963
(You're The) Devil In Disguise	3	1	1963
Please Don't Drag That String Around	-	-	1963
Bossa Nova Baby	8	13	1963
Witchcraft	32	-	1963
Kissin' Cousins	12	10	1964
It Hurts Me	29	-	1964
Kiss Me Quick	34	14	1964
Suspicion	103	-	1964
What I'd Say	21	-	1964
Viva Las Vegas	29	15	1964
Such A Night	16	13	1964
Never Ending	111	-	1964
Ask Me	12	-	1964

Title	US Chart	UK Chart	Year
Ain't That Loving You Baby	16	15	1964
Blue Christmas	1	11	1964
Do The Clam	21	19	1965
You'll Be Gone	121	-	1965
Crying In The Chapel	3	1	1965
(Such An) Easy Question	11	-	1965
It Feels So Right	55	-	1965
I'm Yours	11	-	1965
(It's A) Long Lonely Highway	112	-	1965
Puppet On A String	14	-	1965
Wooden Heart	107	-	1965
Tell Me Why	33	15	1966
Blue River	95	22	1966
Frankie & Johnny	25	21	1966
Please Don't Stop Loving Me	45	-	1966
Love Letters	19	6	1966
Come What May	109	-	1966
Spinout	40	-	1966
All That I Am	41	18	1966
Indescribably Blue	32	21	1967
Fools Fall In Love	102	-	1967
Long Legged Girl (With The Short Dress On)	63	49	1967
That's Someone You Never Forget	92	-	1967
There's Always Me	56	-	1967
Judy	78	-	1967
Big Boss Man	38	-	1967
You Don't Know Me	44	-	1968
Guitar Man	43	19	1968
US Male	28	15	1968
Stay Away	67	-	1968
You'll Never Walk Alone	90	44	1968
We Call On Him	106	-	1968
Your Time Hasn't Come Yet Baby	71	22	1968
Let Yourself Go	72	-	1968
A Little Less Conversation	69	-	1968
Almost In Love	95	-	1968
If I Can Dream	12	11	1968
Edge of Reality	112	-	1969
Memories	35	-	1969

Title	US Chart	UK Chart	Year	Title	US Chart	UK Chart	Year
How Great Thou Art	101	-	1969	The Elvis Medley	71	51	1982
In The Ghetto	3	2	1969	The Sound Of Your Cry	-	59	1982
Clean Up Your Own Back Yard	35	21	1969	Are You Lonesome Tonight?	-	25	1982
Suspicious Minds	1	2	1969	Jailhouse Rock	-	27	1983
Don't Cry Daddy	6	8	1969	Baby I Don't Care	-	61	1983
Kentucky Rain	16	21	1970	I Can Help	-	30	1983
The Wonder Of You	9	1	1970	The Last Farewell	-	48	1984
I've Lost You	32	9	1970	Always On My Mind	-	59	1985
You Don't Have To Say				Ain't That Loving You Baby	-	47	1987
You Love Me	11	9	1970	Love Me Tender	-	56	1987
I Really Don't Want To Know	21	-	1970	Are You Lonesome Tonight?	-	68	1991
There Goes My Everything	-	6	1970	Don't Be Cruel	-	42	1992
Rags To Riches	33	9	1971	The Twelfth of Never	-	21	1995
Life	53	-	1971	Heartbreak Hotel	-	45	1996
I'm Leavin'	36	23	1971	Always On My Mind	-	13	1997
I Just Can't Help Believin'	-	6	1971	Suspicious Minds	-	15	2001
It's Only Love	51	-	1971	America The Beautiful/			
Until It's Time For You To Go	40	5	1972	If I Can Dream	-	69	2001
An American Trilogy	66	8	1972	A Little Less Conversation	50	1	2002
Burning Love	2	7	1972	Rubberneckin'	94	5	2003
Separate Ways	20	-	1972	Blue Moon Of Kentucky/			
Always On My Mind	-	9	1972	That's All Right	-	3	2004
Polk Salad Annie	-	23		Jailhouse Rock/Treat Me Nice	-	1	2005
Fool	-	15		One Night	-	1	2005
Steamroller Blues	17	-	1973	A Fool Such As I	-	2	2005
Raised On Rock	41	36	1973	It's Now Or Never	-	1	2005
I've Got A Thing About You Baby	39	33	1974	Are You Lonesome Tonight?	-	2	2005
If You Talk In Your Sleep	17	40	1974	Wooden Heart	-	2	2005
Promised Land	14	9	1974	Surrender	-	2	2005
My Boy	20	5	1975	(Marie's the Name) His			
T-R-O-U-B-L-E	35	31	1975	Latest Flame	-	3	2005
Bringing It Back	65	-	1975	Rock-a-Hula Baby/Can't Help			
Hurt	28	37	1976	Falling in Love	-	3	2005
Moody Blue	31	6	1976	Good Luck Charm	-	2	2005
Way Down	18	-	1977	She's Not You	-	3	2005
My Way	22	9	1977	Return To Sender	-	5	2005
Softly As I Leave You	109	-	1978	(You're The) Devil In Disguise	-	2	2005
Let Me Be Your Teddy				Crying In The Chapel	-	2	2005
Bear (re-release)	105	-	1978	The Wonder Of You	-	4	2005
Guitar Man	28	-	1981	Way Down	-	2	2005

Title	US Chart	UK Chart	Year
A Little Less Conversation	-	3	2005
Suspicious Minds	-	11	2007
Blue Suede Shoes/Tutti Frutti	-	13	2007
My Baby Left Me	-	19	2007
Hound Dog/Don't Be Cruel	-	14	2007
(Let Me Be Your) Teddy Bear	-	14	2007
Party	-	14	2007
Don't	-	14	2007
Hard Headed Woman	-	15	2007
King Creole	-	15	2007
Big Hunk o' Love	-	12	2007
Where My Ring Around Your Neck	-	16	2007
If I Can Dream	-	17	2007
Viva Las Vegas	-	15	2007
In The Ghetto	-	13	2007
You Don't Have To Say You Love Me	-	16	2007
Always On My Mind	-	17	2007
An American Trilogy	-	12	2007
Blue Christmas	-	195	2007
Burning Love	-	13	2007
Baby Let's Play House	-	84	2008

ALBUMS

Title	Position (US)	Position (UK)	Year
Elvis Presley (Rock 'n' Roll in UK)	1	1	1956
Elvis (Rock 'n' Roll No 2 in UK)	1	3	1956
Love Me Tender (EP OST)	22	-	1956
Peace in the Valley (EP)	3	-	1957
Loving You (OST)	1	1	1957
Elvis' Christmas Album	1	2	1957
Jailhouse Rock (EP)	1	-	1957
Elvis' Golden Records (comp)	3	2	1958
King Creole (OST)	2	1	1958
Elvis Is Back!	2	1	1960
GI Blues (OST)	1	1	1960
His Hand In Mine	13	3	1960
Something For Everybody	1	2	1961
Blue Hawaii (OST)	1	1	1961

Title	Position (US)	Position (UK)	Year
Pot Luck	4	1	1962
Girls! Girls! Girls! (OST*)	3	2	1962
It Happened At The World's Fair (OST)	4	4	1963
Elvis' Golden Records Vol. 3 (comp)	3	6	1963
Fun In Acapulco (OST)	3	9	1963
Kissin' Cousins (OST)	6	5	1964
Roustabout (OST)	1	12	1964
Girl Happy (OST)	8	8	1965
Elvis For Everyone! (comp)	10	8	1965
Harum Scarum (OST) (Harem Holiday in UK)	8	11	1965
Frankie & Johnny (OST)	20	11	1966
Paradise, Hawaiian Style (OST)	15	7	1966
Spinout (OST) (California Holiday in UK)	18	17	1966
How Great Thou Art	18	11	1967
Double Trouble (OST)	47	34	1967
Clambake (OST)	40	39	1967
Elvis (NBC TV Special)	8	2	1968
From Elvis In Memphis	13	1	1969
From Memphis to Vegas, From Vegas to Memphis (2disc)	12	3	1969
On Stage—February 1970	13	2	1970
That's The Way It Is	21	12	1970
Elvis Country	12	6	1971
Love Letters From Elvis	33	7	1971
Elvis: As Recorded At Madison Square Garden (live)	11	3	1972
Elvis Now	43	12	1972
He Touched Me	79	38	1972
Aloha From Hawaii: Via Satellite (live)	1	11	1973
Elvis (1973)	56	16	1973
Elvis: As Recorded Live On Stage In Memphis (live)	33	44	1974
Promised Land	47	21	1975
From Elvis Presley Boulevard, Memphis, Tennessee	41	29	1976
Moody Blue	3	3	1977
Elvis In Concert (live)	5	13	1977

* OST = Original soundtrack

ARE YOU AN ELVIS MASTERMIND?

So you think you know all there is to know about the King of Rock 'n' Roll? Here is your chance to prove it. We present fifty questions, ranging from the relatively easy to the downright brain-teasin', to find out exactly how clued-in you are. Answers on page 4.

1. What was Elvis' twin brother called?
2. In which year did Elvis' mother die?
3. How much did Elvis pay for Graceland?
4. In which year was Elvis' first release on Sun Records?
5. With whom did Elvis form the short-lived Million-Dollar Quartet?
6. What song did Elvis sing that really caught Sun Records boss Sam Philips' ear?
7. What shoe size was Elvis?
8. In which year was his daughter Lisa Marie born?
9. How many tracks has Elvis had inducted into the Grammy Hall of Fame?
10. Where was Elvis' manager Colonel Tom Parker's born?
11. In which year did Elvis win the Grammy Lifetime Achievement Award?
12. Where did Elvis do his army service?
13. What year was "Heartbreak Hotel" inducted into the Grammy Hall of Fame?
14. What is the first track on the first side of Elvis' self-titled debut album?
15. What rank was Elvis discharged from the military with?
16. What was Elvis' only U.S. album to go platinum without charting in the *Billboard* 200?
17. On what TV network was Elvis' 68 *Comeback Special* broadcast?
18. What was Elvis' first album to chart outside of the U.S. Top Ten?
19. What was Elvis's first platinum-selling album?
20. What was the name of Elvis' character in his debut film *Love Me Tender*?
21. What was Elvis' last feature film?
22. How many consecutive weeks did Elvis' *Blue Hawaii* soundtrack stay at Number 1 for?
23. In which year was "Are You Lonesome Tonight" inducted into the Grammy Hall of Fame?
24. What was Elvis' last studio album released in his lifetime?
25. In which year did Elvis win his first Grammy?
26. What was it for?
27. In which year did Elvis marry Priscilla?
28. What was Priscilla's maiden name?
29. From where was *Aloha From Hawaii* broadcast?
30. In what city was Elvis' final concert before his death?
31. What did Elvis ask President Nixon for at their White House meeting in 1970?
32. What year was "Suspicious Minds" inducted into the Grammy Hall of Fame?
33. What year did Elvis leave Sun for RCA Victor?
34. How much was his contract bought out for?
35. What was Elvis' lowest-charting UK album?
36. What year was it released?
37. How many Grammys was Elvis nominated for in his lifetime?
38. Who were in Elvis' early-career backing band, the Blue Moon Boys?
39. How many songs has Elvis has in *Billboard*'s Hot 100 as of 2010?
40. How many of those reached Number 1?
41. What did Elvis win at the 1973 Grammy Awards?
42. What year was "That's All Right (Mama)" inducted into the Grammy Hall of Fame?
43. What year was Graceland put on the National Register of Historic Places?
44. What position did *Double Trouble* soundtrack reach on the *Billboard* 200?
45. According to Box Office Report what was Elvis' top-grossing motion picture?
46. What date was Elvis' funeral?
47. In which year was Elvis' divorce from Priscilla finalized?
48. What award did Elvis' 1972 docufilm *Elvis On Tour* win?
49. What track did Elvis sing to close his 1968 *Comeback Special*?
50. On what street did Elvis live before moving into Graceland?

WHAT'S ON THE CD

1 Hound Dog
Written by Jerry Leiber and Mike Stoller, Elvis recorded the song in July 1956 with Scotty Moore on guitar, Bill Black on bass, D. J. Fontana on drums, and backing vocals from the Jordanaires

2 All Shook Up
Composed by Otis Blackwell, Elvis recorded the song in January 1957. Released in March 1957 it spent eight weeks at the top of the U.S. pop chart.

3 Jailhouse Rock
Another Leiber and Stoller tune, it was released in September 1957 at the same time as the film of the same name. It was a U.S. number one for seven weeks and also topped the UK charts in 1958.

4 Heartbreak Hotel
Released in January 1956, the song was pernned by Tommy Durden and Mae Boren Axton. Elvis' first song for RCA Victor, it was also his first number one. It sold over a million copies and was the best-selling number that year.

5 Don't Be Cruel
Recorded at the same time as b-side "Hound Dog," "Don't be Cruel" was written by Otis Blackwell.

6 It's Now or Never
Released in July 1960 with 'A Mess of Blues' as the b side, this sold twenty-five million records and topped the British and American charts.

7 Are You Lonesome Tonight?
Published originally in 1926, Elvis recorded the song in April 1960. Released in November it spent six week at the top of the U.S. charts.

8 Such A Night
Written by Lincoln Chase and first recorded by The Drifters in 1953, Elvis included the song on his first album. As a single in 1964 it reached 16 in the U.S. and 13 in the U.K.

9 Blue Suede Shoes
Carl Perkins recorded this in 1954 and it quickly became a rock 'n' roll favorite. It was the first track on Elvis' first album but only reached number 20 as a single.

10 King Creole
Written by Leiber and Stoller, this song is the title track on Elvis' sixth album, which featured songs from the movie of the same name. It reached number two in the charts.

11 Long Tall Sally
A RnR classic, written and initially recorded by Little Richard, Elvis included it on his second album, released in 1956.

12 Rip It Up
Written by Robert Blackwell and John Marascalco, Elvis included it on his second album, released in 1956.

INDEX